HOW TO SELL A LOBSTER

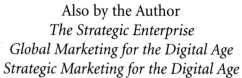

Also by the Author
The Strategic Enterprise
Global Marketing for the Digital Age
Strategic Marketing for the Digital Age

How to Sell A Lobster

THE MONEY-MAKING SECRETS OF A STREETWISE ENTREPRENEUR

Bill Bishop

KEY PORTER BOOKS

Library and Archives Canada Cataloguing in Publication

Bishop, Bill, 1957–
    How to sell a lobster : the money-making secrets of a streetwise
entrepreneur / Bill Bishop.

ISBN 1-55263-759-X

    1. Marketing. 2. Selling. 3. Success in business. I. Title.

HF5386.B468 2006   658.8   C2005-906551-6

The Canada Council | Le Conseil des Arts
for the arts | du Canada
since 1957 | depuis 1957

ONTARIO ARTS COUNCIL
CONSEIL DES ARTS DE L'ONTARIO

The publisher gratefully acknowledges the support of the Canada Council for the Arts and
the Ontario Arts Council for its publishing program. We acknowledge the support of the
Government of Ontario through the Ontario Media Development Corporation's Ontario
Book Initiative.

We acknowledge the financial support of the Government of Canada through the Book
Publishing Industry Development Program (BPIDP) for our publishing activities.

Key Porter Books Limited
Six Adelaide Street East, Tenth Floor
Toronto, Ontario
Canada M5C 1H6

www.keyporter.com

Text design and electronic formatting: Martin Gould

Photo of lobster on pages 1, 2 and 3: Corbis Images

Printed and bound in Canada

06 07 08 09 10 5 4 3 2 1

*For my mother
Priscilla*

Contents

A Series of Fortunate Events

Ever since I was a kid, I had never been able to get a rise out of my uncle. A generally quiet fellow and a lawyer by trade, my uncle always maintained a pretty even keel. But one night at a family dinner party, I got him laughing uproariously. I was telling him about how I employed a special marketing trick years before to sell more than 1400 lobsters in a waitering contest. He thought the story was hilarious.

"I can't believe you did that!" he said between gasps and guffaws. "It's outrageous! It's ridiculous! And it really worked? That's amazing." My uncle was incredulous, but he was also quite impressed. I had touched a nerve.

That's when the lightening bolt of inspiration struck. I thought, if my uncle thinks the lobster story is funny and enlightening, then other people might think so too. Perhaps I could write a humorous book about the lobster contest and other key moments in my life when I learned an important lesson about sales and marketing. Maybe it could be a different kind of book from the three more academic books I had written previously and from all the other business books out there already. Right then and there I decided to write a book called *How to Sell a Lobster*.

From the start I knew *How to Sell a Lobster* could be no ordinary book. After all, I had led no ordinary life. I had done a lot of things that many people find surprising—and sometimes a little unsettling.

It all started when I was eight years old. Some pals and I were rummaging through some boxes in a back alley when we discovered a big crate of calendars. Although it was July, and the year was more than half spent, I was convinced we could sell the calendars, and use the cash to buy some candy and make other important purchases.

We set up a little booth and positioned ourselves on the sidewalk at a busy intersection. I made a bright red sign that read: "Calendars For Sale. 10 cents." But after about half an hour, we had sold only three measly calendars, so I changed the sign. Now it read: "Special Calendar Sale. Two For One. Only 20 cents. Get Them Before They Are Gone." We also enlisted my friend's little sister Suzie—who was really adorable—as our sales representative.

The change in our fortunes was immediate and dramatic. The adults walking by thought the sign was hilarious, and they thought Suzie was really cute. Within two hours we had sold 200 calendars and pocketed a cool $20, which we spent just as quickly on a hearty feast of bubble gum, suckers, and Cracker Jacks.

That was just the beginning of something big. At the age of ten, I worked after school at my parents' marketing company. For $1.65 an hour, I stuffed envelopes and fooled around with the office equipment. One Friday afternoon, the postage meter man caught me red-handed, launching paper airplanes by stuffing them through the new electric postage machine. He was really angry and threatened to confiscate the equipment, but I thought it was really funny, and frankly a darn good idea.

When I turned thirteen, my parents gave me a much-deserved promotion, and offered me a 25-cent raise if I would help them with a retail promotion they were running. Resplendently attired in a gargantuan frog mask and bright green, sequined tuxedo, I patrolled a local shopping mall, handing out balloons and prizes to shoppers and their children. It was an utterly degrading assignment, but I hid my embarrassment beneath my amphibian mask.

But that was not to be the end of my debasement. The following spring, I found myself in the same mall dressed as a pink bunny rabbit, doling out Easter candies from a little handbasket. This gender-bending gig, which took twenty years of intense therapy to overcome, convinced me to explore the world of business and to try to find a better way to make a buck.

Although it didn't seem that way at the time, a series of fortunate events ensued. My next job was washing hundreds of smelly, greasy pots during interminable ten-hour shifts. Next, I spent two weeks making and selling candy floss at a summer carnival. Then I sold hot dogs at an amusement park, followed by a job hawking newspapers on a street corner. I also prowled my neighbourhood raking leaves, shovelling snow, and doing odd jobs for little old ladies. These forms of employment occupied me until the age of fifteen.

I don't know why I was so motivated and ambitious at such an early age. A lot of these jobs were really hard and some of them were disgusting. (Believe me, if you ever handle candy floss for two straight weeks, you will understand the true meaning of disgusting.) But something told me that all of these work experiences were leading somewhere. I could tell that each job was teaching me something, but at such a young age I wasn't sure what the lessons were.

Over the next decade, I had scores of other jobs. I worked as a movie usher, a chauffeur, an oven cleaner, a ski-lift operator, a tennis instructor, and a computer operator. Then I got a job working as a waiter, and achieved immortality of a sort by selling many, many lobsters. This episode, which is fully documented in Chapter One, taught me an important lesson about packaging and marketing.

Following graduation from journalism school at the age of twenty-five, I discovered that newspaper jobs were scarce so I decided to start a community magazine with a friend of mine. As a two-man operation, we learned fast what it takes to run your own business. We worked hard and made no money, but we had a great time.

Two years later, I decided to give up the magazine and get a real job. I went to work at a corporate PR company and hated every minute of it. I hated the office politics and the long, boring meetings. By the time I left two years later, I even hated the colour of the walls. I knew I had to be my own boss, even if that meant a life of starvation and penury. So I started my own marketing company, which is now called Bishop Information Group or BIG for short.

Things got off to a scary start. The day after I quit my job, the stock market crashed. That was October 1987, and I thought I had made the biggest mistake of my life. But I was wrong. Starting my own business was the best decision of my life. Since that time, my partner, Curtis Verstraete, and I have worked with more than 4,000 business people from just about every type of company and industry. We've helped them develop some really big ideas to get more customers and make more money—sometimes a lot more money.

From my years as a business and marketing coach, I've learned a thousand things that don't work, and a handful of things that work really well. I've also learned that the world has completely changed. With the advent of free trade, computers, and the Internet, the old ways of doing things just don't work anymore. All of the lessons we learned in school, and at the knees of our kin, are no longer working. In this post-industrial age, we need to entertain new ideas and explore new ways of doing things. We need to turn everything on its ear and become more entrepreneurial. We need to learn new ways to sell lobsters.

I also know that no one needs another boring business book. Let's face it, most business people don't want to wade through a long, dreary book by some marketing professor. They want to know what works and what doesn't from someone who has been in the trenches, fighting the good fight. They want to learn from a street-smart entrepreneur— someone who knows exactly what they are going through.

That's why this book is short, fun, and easy to digest. Each chapter is a parable about a real-life business problem, and how my trusted mentor, Marketing Mike, and I used an unusual and innovative approach to solve that problem. The stories are self-contained, but they also build upon each other. They are some of the many stories I've told my clients and speaking audiences for years and years.

Looking back over all these decades, I'm really glad I had all of those different jobs. Each job taught me something new and valuable. By getting my hands dirty and trying everything at least once, I learned what it takes to start a new business venture, get new customers, make a sale, and turn a profit.

I've learned that you sometimes have to take bold action and do something outlandish if you want to succeed. I've also learned that understanding what makes people tick is essential to success in business.

But most of all, I've learned that you have to have fun. Without a spirit of play, a good sense of humour, and a taste for the unexpected, I contend that your business will probably flounder in today's super-competitive and increasingly crowded marketplace. I've learned that sometimes you have to dress up like a frog or an Easter bunny and hand out balloons. Otherwise, no one will notice you.

So let's get going. Let's start by learning how to sell lobsters—and lots of them.

ONE

How to Sell a Lobster

When I look back over my multifarious career with all its twists and turns, I shudder to think that I could still be working as a salad bar attendant had not the fates intervened on my behalf.

Back in the early '80s while I was studying journalism, I spent my evenings slicing pickles and cleaning lettuce at a popular steak restaurant in Toronto. As a newcomer at the establishment, I started off as the lowly salad bar attendant, but that suited me just fine.

At that time, I had limited ambition. I just wanted to cut up vegetables in the kitchen, listen to music on the radio, and fool around with the dishwashers. But after six months of vegetarian bliss, my complacency came to an abrupt end when the manager asked me if I wanted to become a waiter.

"Who me?" I replied, making no effort to hide my terror. "You want me to be a waiter?" I trembled at the prospect. If I took the promotion, I would have to face customers. Real people. I would have to talk to them and take their orders.

"What if I make a fool of myself?" I worried. "What will I do if they have a complaint?"

But I couldn't back out. There were kids five years younger than me working as waiters. Besides, waiters made ten times more money than salad bar attendants, and the cocktail waitresses were a lot prettier than the guys working in the kitchen.

So, reluctantly, I became a waiter. And I began by screwing up royally. I dropped a plate of rice into the lap of my very first customer. But I learned quickly, and within a few months I had become a competent waiter. I learned how to deal with people face to face. Hundreds of them. Night after night. I learned to juggle ten tables at once and take care of special requests. I learned how to mollify obnoxious patrons. I even tackled one guy running full gallop down the street who had tried to get away without paying his bill. Within no time, I thought I had the waiter game all figured out. That is, until the management launched The Great Lobster Contest.

The Great Lobster Contest was designed to boost the sales of lobster "add-ons" at the restaurant. Add-ons are secondary menu items—such as baked potatoes, vegetables, and seafood—which customers can order in addition to their steak.

To sell more add-ons, we were encouraged to use "suggestive selling." We were told to ask customers, "Would you like a baked potato or some crab legs with your steak?" "Would you like some delicious cheesecake for dessert?" I never liked suggestive selling because I thought it was too pushy, but I tried it. Sometimes it worked, and sometimes it didn't.

Management, however, wasn't satisfied with the sales of lobster add-ons, so they launched the contest. The waiter who sold the most lobsters over a three-month period would win a prize.

"How do we get more people to buy lobsters?" I asked the restaurant manager.

"Just make sure you use suggestive selling, and ask every customer if they want a lobster with their steak," he told me.

So for the next two weeks I asked every customer if they wanted a lobster with their steak. The response was usually negative: "Nope." "No thanks." "Not tonight, thank you." "What do you think we are? Rich?"

At the end of each night, the manager asked me how many lobsters I'd sold. "Three, one, four, none," I said sheepishly. Obviously, I wasn't doing very well, but fortunately for me none of the other waiters were selling very many lobsters either. But I was eager to make a breakthrough; I just didn't know what to do to sell more lobsters.

Then I had a lucky break that changed everything, not just in the contest, but in my life. I met Marketing Mike.

A friend of my father, Marketing Mike was a highly successful businessman with decades of experience in sales and marketing. "Why don't you visit him and see if he has any ideas on how you can sell more lobsters?" my dad suggested.

I didn't think Marketing Mike would be interested in meeting a young kid with a seafood sales problem, but he readily agreed to meet me at the restaurant before work. When I told him about The Great Lobster Contest, Marketing Mike said, "The problem is, you and the other waiters are trying too hard to *sell* lobsters when you should be trying to *market* lobsters instead."

"What do you mean?"

"Most people in business are sales oriented. They create a product or service, bang on doors, make their sales pitch, and hope for the best. Just like you do with the lobsters. Your manager tells you to use suggestive selling, but it isn't working. And it isn't working because you haven't taken the time to think about what's going on inside the customer's mind."

"But how do I know what's going on inside the customer's mind?" I asked.

"Start by thinking like your customer," Marketing Mike said. "Start by thinking like a marketer instead of a salesperson."

"What's the difference between sales and marketing?"

"Sales is when you knock on someone's door, trying to make a sale. And marketing is when you do something to get customers to knock on *your* door."

"So how do you get customers to knock on your door?" I asked.

"By playing *marketing games* instead of *sales games*," he replied.

"What are marketing games?"

"They are marketing strategies and tactics you can use with your customers and prospects to increase your sales and grow your business."

"But aren't marketing games bad? Aren't they kind of sneaky and underhanded?"

"Let's not forget that business is a game," Marketing Mike said. "And the goal of the game is to get customers to buy something. First of all, to play this game properly, you should play to win. And to win you have to use strategies and tactics.

"Secondly, to get better at the game, you also have to be willing to take risks and try new things. To play marketing games, you have to keep trying until you find the tactics and strategies that work.

"And thirdly, it all depends on your motivation and integrity. If you don't care about your customers, and you just want to make a sale no matter what, then you are playing a bad game. And you'll probably lose. But if you are really trying to help people, then you are playing a good game. And you'll probably win."

"So what kind of marketing game can we play to get people to buy more lobsters?"

"Well, the first thing to do is to think like the typical customer at your restaurant. Try to see the situation from their perspective."

"Okay, how do we do that?"

"Well, it seems to me that a lot of people who eat at a restaurant are the guest of someone else who is going to pay the bill. Isn't that right?"

"Sure."

"If you are a guest of someone, and the waiter asks you if you want a lobster with your steak, you will probably say no because you don't want to look greedy."

"That's right," I said. "You don't want to look like a pig, trying to get as much as you can because someone else is paying. So you just order the smallest steak or the cheapest thing on the menu."

"But it's probably okay to order the special if you are a guest, isn't it?"

"Well, yes. A lot of people do order the special."

"So why don't we create a special that includes a lobster with the steak."

"What do you mean, 'create' a special?"

"I mean, create something new. For example, how much does it cost if someone buys a steak, a lobster, and a side order of rice?"

"It would cost, let me see, $18.50."

"So why don't we tell people we are offering a special for $18.50, which includes a steak, a lobster, and rice."

"How can I do that? The managers make up the specials."

"Well, if you can sell more lobsters, I'm sure the

managers wouldn't care if you made up your own special."

"That's true."

"So are you willing to give this marketing game a try?"

"Okay. I'll try it."

The next night, I walked up to the first table—a group of eight people—and announced that we had a special: a steak, lobster, and rice for $18.50.

Then I asked them what they wanted to order, and the answers floored me. "I'll have the special." "Me too." "I'll have the lobster, too." "The special, please."

I couldn't believe it. Everyone ordered the special. I sold eight lobsters on my first try. And that wasn't the end of the story. That night I sold fifty-eight lobsters. My nearest competitor in the contest sold three.

Excited, I returned to Marketing Mike because I wanted to understand fully why I was selling more lobsters.

"It's simple, really," he said. "Three things are going on. One, people like specials. They sound like more fun. They sound unique and fleeting—a once-in-a-lifetime opportunity that you don't want to miss.

"Second, by combining three menu items into a single idea—the special—the customers can now visualize one small, tidy package in their mind. Instead of reading over the whole menu, they can now make a quick and easy buying decision by choosing the special.

"The third thing is this: by making lobster part of the special, you've given all of the guests permission to get what they really want—a lobster—without looking greedy.

"So," Marketing Mike finished, "everyone wins. The guests get what they want, the host at the table feels more generous, your restaurant makes more money, and you make more tips."

Marketing Mike was right. Over the next three months, the lobster marketing game worked like a charm. I sold more than 1400 lobsters. The second-place finisher sold only ninety.

I was written up in the restaurant's national newsletter as the greatest lobster salesperson in the history of the company. I became the poster boy for the power and potential of add-on sales.

"How did he do it?" everyone wondered. And the fun thing was I never let the secret out of the bag. Until now, that is.

TWO

The First-Member Trap

In spite of my success in The Great Lobster Contest, I was not destined for a lifetime working in a restaurant. Following my graduation from journalism school, I searched for a job at a newspaper. But times were tough, and few positions were available. So I decided to start a community magazine with a friend of mine. We called it *The Uptown* because it served the uptown area of our city.

As writers, we started *The Uptown* because we wanted to write. But we quickly realized that selling advertising was the real business of publishing a magazine. Without ads, there would be no articles to write. We also realized we needed to show advertisers something tangible if we expected them to advertise in the first issue. So we created a mock-up of the magazine, displaying a few dummy articles and empty spaces where advertisers could place their ads.

With our mock-up magazine in hand, we visited the local business and restaurant owners in the area. We showed them the mock-up and described the audience our magazine would reach. We also presented our rate card, which explained the prices for the different ad sizes. The prospects seemed to like the idea of a local entertainment magazine, and they liked our mock-up. But after a week of sales calls, we hadn't sold a single ad. It seemed like a good time to visit Marketing Mike.

"What do you think we're doing wrong?" I asked him, feeling a little depressed.

"You aren't doing anything wrong," Marketing Mike said. "You've produced a beautiful mock-up of your magazine. You're targeting an audience that isn't served by any other publication in your area. And you're offering something really valuable. But there is just one problem."

"What's that?"

"No one wants to be the first advertiser."

"Why not?"

"Well, it's like trying to start a club. No one wants to be the first member. I call this 'The First-Member Trap.'"

"A trap?" I didn't quite understand.

"I call it a trap because you can't get members if you don't have the first one, but you can't get the first member if you don't have members. People don't want to become the first member because they worry they might look like an idiot if no one else joins. Remember, most people are followers, not leaders."

"So how do we get our club started if no one will be the first member?"

"You have to escape from The First-Member Trap.

You need to create the impression that you already have members. And you have to get prospects worried that they may miss out on becoming a member altogether."

"How will we do that?"

"Well, let's think about the situation in your market area. Are there two big restaurants that compete against each other?"

"Sure. Poncho's Restaurant competes for customers against The Big Dish."

"Okay, then. This is what I suggest you do," Marketing Mike said. "Make up a full-page dummy ad for Poncho's Restaurant and put it in your mock-up. Then go see the owner of The Big Dish, and report back to me about what happened."

Following Marketing Mike's advice, my partner and I designed a dummy ad for Poncho's Restaurant and inserted it in the mock-up. Then we went to see the owner of The Big Dish to make our sales pitch.

"Here is our new magazine called *The Uptown*, and this is a mock-up of the first issue," I said, slowly flipping through the pages.

The owner of The Big Dish stopped me when I reached the page displaying the Poncho's ad. He stared at the ad, reading over every detail.

"How much does a full-page ad cost?" he asked.

"Fifteen hundred dollars a month," I said.

"How much does a colour ad cost?"

"Twenty-eight hundred dollars plus production costs."

"I would like to buy a full-page colour ad," he said.

Doing my best to hide my utter astonishment, I processed the paperwork and accepted his cheque for $2800.

"I can't believe he bought an ad," I exclaimed later to Marketing Mike. "I still can't figure out why it happened."

"It's quite easy to understand," Marketing Mike said. "When the owner of The Big Dish saw the ad for Poncho's, he got scared that he was missing out on something big. And he didn't want his competitor to beat him out."

"But we haven't even sold an ad to Poncho's."

"We never said we did. We just gave him a glimpse of what the magazine would look like with his competitor's ad in it. He just assumed you had already sold the ad and that he wouldn't have to be the first member."

"So what do we do now?"

"Now you can take out the dummy ad for Poncho's, make up the real ad for The Big Dish, and put it in your mock-up. Then go and see the owner of Poncho's."

We did what Marketing Mike suggested. During the presentation at Poncho's, the owner stared at the colour ad for The Big Dish and asked, "How much does a two-page ad cost?"

"That would be $3600 for black and white, and $5600 for colour."

"I'll take a two-page colour ad," he said immediately.

Over the next few weeks, we added more ads to our mock-up and continued making sales. Within six weeks, we had enough advertising for our first issue, which was published to great acclaim from both readers and advertisers.

Over coffee, Marketing Mike and I discussed The First-Member Trap to learn more from our experience.

"When you start a new venture, you've got to prime the pump," Marketing Mike said. "In this case, we got The Big Dish to advertise because they thought Poncho's had already bought an ad, and they didn't want to miss out. Then we got Poncho's to take an ad because The Big Dish had already bought one. And once we had the pump primed, the rest of the sales just started to flow.

"In other words," Marketing Mike added, "we created the impression that we already had at least one member, so no one thought they had to be the first. And once we actually *had* a member, the rest of the bunch found it a lot easier to join the club."

"I learned something else important, too," I said. "We replaced the prospect's fear of being the first with the fear of missing out. In this case, it was the fear of missing out to a competitor."

Over the next two years, *The Uptown* prospered. We sold all the ads for each issue. The revenue we generated gave us the opportunity to publish the magazine and write lots of articles. And it was all because we learned how to avoid The First-Member Trap.

THREE

The Lineup

After more than two years publishing the magazine—
working twelve hours a day, seven days a week—we
folded the publication, and I started a marketing-
consulting company. One of my first clients was a
brand new restaurant and nightclub called Todd's
Palace. I had known Todd, the owner, for years. He
was excited about his new venture, but also really
nervous.

After one month in business, his restaurant was
almost completely empty. He was losing money by
the barrel.

"I don't understand this," Todd bemoaned. "I've
got a great location, great food, great staff, and
beautiful décor. I just don't know what else to do."

"Have you done anything to promote your place?"
I asked.

"I was thinking about advertising in the paper
and sending out flyers in the neighbourhood," Todd
said. "A friend of mine suggested I put up posters in
the area, too. Do you think these are good ideas?"

"Advertising and special promotions may work,"

I said. "But maybe we should start by thinking first about your customers and prospects."

"But I don't have any customers," he sighed, placing his head in his hands.

"Well, let's think like the customer anyway. Let's imagine what it's like for someone to walk past your restaurant when no one is inside. Do you like going into a restaurant when there aren't any customers?"

"I hate that," Todd exclaimed. "There's nothing worse than sitting in an empty restaurant. It feels cold and depressing. You figure the food and service must be bad if no one else is there. So you don't go in."

"That's right. No one wants to go into an empty restaurant."

"So what do we do to get people to come in if we don't have any customers?" Todd asked.

"I'll think about it and get back to you," I said, realizing that this was a job for Marketing Mike.

"You're absolutely right," Marketing Mike said later that day. "People hate going into an empty restaurant. They want to go to a busy place."

"So how do we get the ball rolling at Todd's Palace?"

During the next hour, Marketing Mike laid out a marketing game so outrageous that I could hardly believe my ears.

"Are you willing to give it a try?" he asked.

"Well, I'm willing to give it a go, but I'm not sure Todd will buy it."

The next day, I met with Todd and laid out the marketing game.

"My mentor, Marketing Mike, recommends against advertising and promotions," I said, starting off slowly. "He thinks you should save your money and spend it doing two things: give away free drinks and dinners, and start a lineup."

"What do you mean, 'give away free drinks and dinner?'"

"We've got to get people into the restaurant so other people will come in. Marketing Mike suggests we give away free meals and drinks for two weeks."

"Are you kidding? That will cost a fortune."

"Well, you're losing money right now, and you don't have anything to show for it. Besides, it won't cost any more than the advertising you were thinking about buying."

"That's true."

"The key is to give the free drinks and dinners to the right people."

"Like who?"

"Like athletes, models, flight attendants, celebrities, and important business people. Let's invite them to experience Todd's Palace for free."

"Okay. I understand that. But will they come?"

"If we invite thousands of them, hundreds will show up."

"I get that, too, but what's this business about starting a lineup?"

"Well, Marketing Mike suggests that we pay

people to stand in line out front."

"Why would I want to do that?"

"Because if people see a lineup, they figure something big is happening and they will want to get in on it."

"I get it," Todd said triumphantly. "If we create a lineup, people will want to get in, so they'll join the line, too. And that will make even more people join the line. And it will go on and on."

"Marketing Mike says people want things that appear popular more than they want things that are not popular. So the trick is to create an aura of popularity. That's what The Lineup does for your restaurant."

After more discussion and planning, Todd agreed to play the marketing game. I gave him a lot of credit because he was taking a big risk and was making a commitment to spend a lot of money giving away free value. But Todd also knew he had to do something dramatic because the downside was even scarier.

Over the next few weeks, we distributed invitations (with free food and drink vouchers) to all the modelling agencies, sports clubs, radio and TV stations, newspapers, and airlines in town. We also mailed invitations to prominent professionals, important business owners, and local celebrities.

Then we hired twenty people to act as liner-uppers. We taught them how to stand in line and look anxious and excited. We also hired a bouncer with really big muscles to guard the door.

On the first night, about three dozen people showed up. Our liner-uppers worked their way through the line, got into the restaurant, and then ten minutes later, went out the back door. They joined the line in front once again. And sure enough, the lineup started to draw people in.

"I wonder what's going on in there?" passersby asked. "Look at all the good-looking girls," one man said to another. "Did you see that really cute guy?" a woman asked a friend as they joined the line.

That first night, Todd gave away a lot of free food and drinks, but he also made a lot of sales to other customers who were drawn in by the sense of excitement. In fact, he sold three times as many meals as he had on any previous night.

Over the next week, the whole process accelerated. More and more VIPs showed up, and the lineup got longer and longer. People driving by stopped to find out what all the excitement was about. We had to hire an off-duty police officer to manage the traffic in the adjacent parking lot. Todd had to bring on extra waiters and bartenders to handle the influx.

By the second week, we no longer needed our paid liner-uppers. We had real people in our line now, and we didn't need to send out any more free invitations. We were getting enough real customers.

"I can't believe this," Todd kept saying to himself. "All this business has more than paid for the free stuff we gave away. We've also been featured on television and in the newspapers. This is great."

To celebrate, Todd invited Marketing Mike and me to dinner at his restaurant. During the meal, we asked Marketing Mike why The Lineup marketing game works.

"Most businesses never get off the ground because they don't get the ball rolling," he said. "They think advertising and flyers and hot-air balloons are going to do the trick. But most of the time they are wasting their money."

"It's a lot cheaper to give away something of value to get them in the door for the first time. It generates a lot of excitement and word of mouth. It also projects the impression that your business is a vibrant and successful enterprise right from the start."

"But what about the lineup?" Todd asked. "How did that work again?"

"By creating our own lineup, we projected the impression that people were willing to wait to get into your restaurant. That communicated the idea that your restaurant *must* be great. And once other people got into the lineup, it became self-generating."

"Can this work in other businesses besides restaurants?" Todd asked.

"Of course," Marketing Mike replied. "The Lineup will work in every business. If you create an impression that people are lining up or waiting to buy your product or receive your service, more people will want it. You simply have to establish an aura of popularity and exclusiveness. In other words, don't necessarily make it easy for people to get your product or service. Make them line up first."

"I never thought of it that way before," Todd said.

"That's because you were thinking like a salesperson instead of playing marketing games."

Over the next months and years, Todd's Palace prospered. The Lineup got the ball rolling—and it just kept on going. And for more than ten years, there was a lineup in front of Todd's Palace every night.

FOUR

The Three Boxes

To augment my income as a marketing consultant, I started selling advertising for a local high-end lifestyle magazine. As the former publisher of a community magazine, I thought I knew all about selling ad space. But I was wrong. I hadn't learned how to use The Three Boxes.

My lesson started the first day on the job when the advertising manager explained the assignment.

"We want you to sell ads in our small retailers section," she said. "Each ad costs $300 a month. We suggest you call on retailers, show them our magazine, and explain the value of reaching our affluent readers."

At the time, I didn't realize I was at the bottom of the advertising food chain. No one else wanted to sell these little ads to small retailers because no one had ever sold enough of them to make a living. But I didn't think it would be too hard. I figured it was a numbers game. The more retailers I called, the more ads I would sell. So I opened up the *Yellow*

Pages and started calling every retailer in the city.

My telephone pitch was simple: "Hi, my name is Bill Bishop. I'm calling from — *Magazine.* We have a special ad section for retailers like yourself."

In most cases, I was able to get only that much out of my mouth before someone slammed down the telephone. It was discouraging and humiliating, but I figured out another way to do it: a unique tele-marketing method I called "The Hang-Up-First Technique."

I would call a retailer and say, "Hi. Can I speak to the person who handles your advertising?" If the person on the other end merely grunted, or groaned, or moaned, or acted in any way surly or nasty, I just hung up!

To maintain my dignity and take control of the situation, I had decided to hang up on them before they got a chance to hang up on me. It was really empowering. I hung up on dozens of prospects that first day.

Within a week, I had further developed my own scientific way to make telemarketing calls. My goal was to dial the telephone fifty times every morning and set up five afternoon appointments. If they were about to hang up on me, I simply hung up on them. This sped up the process and gave me a greater sense of power. Then in the afternoon I would visit the retailers in person. And it worked. I was meeting with more than twenty retailers a week.

But there was only one problem. I couldn't sell an ad if my life depended on it.

I would show them the magazine—one of the most widely read and well-respected magazines in the country. I would show them the ad and explain the costs. And invariably they would say, "No. No. No. No."

Obviously, it was time for a visit to Marketing Mike. And, of course, he saw the problem right away.

"You are doing almost everything right," Marketing Mike said. "You know that telemarketing is a numbers game. The more people you call, the more people you will meet, and the greater the chances you will make a sale. I'm not so sure about this hanging-up business, but if it works for you, then go for it. You are getting in to see the retailers, and that's good. But you've got one problem."

"What's that?"

"You're offering them only one size of ad."

"That's what they've given me to sell," I explained. "I have only one size."

"Well, if you want to sell ads, or anything else for that matter, you have to offer more than one size. Three sizes, in fact."

"Why's that?" I asked.

"Let me tell you a story," Marketing Mike said. "When I was a little kid, I would go to the movies. I usually got a drink, and the guy behind the counter would always ask, 'Would you like a large or a small one?'"

"I ordered a small drink, and my mother ordered a small drink too because she was on a diet. And as it turned out, eighty percent of the customers at the theatre always ordered the small drink.

"Now this went on for many years at every theatre. Eighty percent of the people bought the small size and twenty percent bought the large size. This pattern continued until the early 1980s when theatre owners tried to figure out how to get more people to order the large drink.

"Then someone suggested that they introduce a third size, a supersize, to see if that would change anything. So the question is: if you go to a theatre now and order the largest drink, how big is it?"

"It's huge," I said. "You can't drink it all."

"That's right. It's absolutely massive. And do you know why they sell this huge third size?"

"Why?"

"Because now twenty percent of people buy the small size, sixty percent of customers buy the regular size—which is actually the old large—and twenty percent of people buy the supersize, which theatre owners never anticipated. So now they have eighty percent of the people ordering either the old large or an even larger size. All because they introduced the third choice—the supersize."

"How does that work?" I asked, starting to get thirsty.

"Well, it has to do with human nature. If you sell one size—which most people do—then the customer has a choice between only 'yes' and 'no.' And because they don't have anything else to think about, they focus on the price. They try to get you to lower it."

"You mean they're more likely to haggle if you offer only one size."

"That's right. Now if you have two sizes, that's better. The customers are choosing between the small and the large, so they're more likely to buy something. There's one problem: Most people will choose the small size."

"Why's that?"

"Because most people think small, or they are trying to save money. Or they are cautious because they aren't sure if they are making the right decision. So they play it safe and buy the small. In fact, it is almost always eighty percent small when you offer only two sizes."

"That's interesting," I said.

"If you have three sizes, however, the whole game changes. Customers will start by looking at the large size first, or the most expensive or most elaborate offering. They will look at it first because it is so dazzling, so beautiful, so huge. Then they will look at the price and realize it is way out of their league. So they will then look at the small size. But the small size doesn't look so great compared with the supersize. It looks cheap, small, and unappealing."

"So then they look at the middle size," Mike continued, "and that looks just right. It's not too small or too large. It's not too cheap or too expensive. And because it is called the *regular*, it is also the safe bet because it means that it is the one most people buy."

"Like you say," I chimed in, "most people are followers, not leaders."

"That's right. Most people will buy the middle box because it is the one most people buy. So here's the trick: If you have something you want to sell most of the time, position it in the middle, make a small version, and a supersize version, and most people will buy the one in the middle."

"But what about the supersize? Why do some people buy that one?"

"Well, that's the bonus of using The Three Boxes marketing game. Most people will buy the regular middle box, but some people will go for the supersize. And the irony is, you weren't even expecting to sell the supersize. You simply created it to get more people to buy the middle one."

"That's totally cool," I said, abandoning any pretense of sophistication.

"There are other features that make The Three Boxes marketing game even cooler," Marketing Mike added. "By adding the pricey supersize option, you can also charge more for the regular size."

"How does that work?"

"Let's say you were going to charge five dollars

for your regular size. Well now you can charge ten dollars because the supersize costs a hundred dollars."

"I see. The ten-dollar size will look reasonably priced compared with the hundred dollar super-size."

"You've got it. So you can make more money. As well, by using this marketing game, no one will ever say you charge too much."

"How come?"

"Because you aren't actually charging too much. You are just giving them a choice. The customer has to decide if they are the kind of person who drives a Volkswagen, a Cadillac, or a Rolls Royce. It is all about them, and not about you. They have to decide what kind of person they are—and want to become."

"I see how this can work with drinks at a movie theatre, but does it work in other businesses too?"

"The Three Boxes marketing game will work in every business. It will work with watches, travel packages, fast food, consulting services, diapers, and private jets. The principles are universal. You just have to spend the time developing the three boxes."

"So what should I do with my ads?" I asked.

"What do you think you should do?" Marketing Mike asked back.

"I guess I should create three sizes of ads, and sell those instead of just one."

"You've got it. Are you willing to give this marketing game a try?" Mike asked.

"Absolutely."

So the next day I met with the advertising manager and worked out the sizing and pricing of the three ads. That afternoon, I visited my retail prospects.

"So here are your three choices for ads," I said. "Basic, regular, and extra-large."

Right away, I could see the difference in the prospects. Instead of haggling with me over the price of a single size of ad, they spent a few minutes looking at the three sizes and three prices, trying to decide which one to choose.

"I'll take the regular size," the first prospect said. "I'll take the regular size," the second prospect said. "I'll go for the extra-large size," the third one said.

Once again, I couldn't believe my ears. The Three Boxes marketing game worked just like Marketing Mike said it would. Over the next two weeks, I sold more than two ads every day. Back at the magazine, they were amazed. They couldn't believe all the sales I was making. Nobody could.

I took Marketing Mike out for dinner to review the power of The Three Boxes marketing game.

"The game works because you are giving your customers and prospects a choice. That's what marketing is all about—choice. Let the customers make up their own minds. As well, it's important to remember that the number three is critical. Otherwise you might be tempted to give people four choices."

"Well, why not?" I asked. "Wouldn't four boxes give the customer even more choice?"

"Yes, they get more choice. But too many choices can be overwhelming. They might not be able to make up their mind. As well, with four boxes there is no middle."

"What do you mean, no middle?"

"With four boxes, you can't choose the one in the middle, so it's harder to make the easy, safe choice. With four boxes, people tend to get confused. And if they get confused, they might not buy anything at all."

I've never forgotten Marketing Mike's lesson about The Three Boxes. I've used it hundreds of times myself and with my clients. I've also noticed that lots of savvy marketers use The Three Boxes. And here's an interesting thing: Even though I know all about The Three Boxes, and all about the game they are playing with me, I invariably buy the regular box, the middle box.

So why don't you give it a try? You may find it works for you, too.

FIVE

The Captain
of the TITANIC

Over the years, working as a marketing consultant, I've come across just about every kind of company. I've worked with dentists, electricians, software companies, clown acts, morticians, life insurance agents, and toilet bowl sanitation experts. This experience has taught me that all businesses have the same objectives. They all want to make more money from their existing customers; attract new, high-quality customers; and increase their profit margins.

I've also learned that many companies do not achieve these goals. Why? Because they focus on making sales and meeting quotas, instead of building long-term relationships with their customers.

Marketing Mike captured the problem. "Most salespeople really don't care very much about their customers," he explained. "They just care about themselves. They don't care if people really need their product as long as they can sell it to someone."

"I certainly know a lot of salespeople like that," I agreed.

"We all do," Marketing Mike went on. "It reminds me of the story about the captain of the *Titanic*."

"Which story?" I asked.

"Well, let's pretend you're selling lifeboats, and you approach the captain of the *Titanic* just before the ship sails. You ask the captain if he needs lifeboats. And, of course, he says no—because he thinks he has an unsinkable ship. But you're a salesperson, and naturally you want to sell him something. So you ask him if he has any other needs. He says he's concerned that he'll run out of champagne in the first-class dining room. So instead of selling him lifeboats, which you know he needs desperately, you sell him some champagne."

"What's wrong with that?" I asked. "Isn't that what a salesperson is supposed to do: sell the customer something?"

"Well, yes and no. It's important to make sales, but you need to make the right sales to the right people."

"Why is that?" I asked. As usual, I was intrigued.

"Well, think about it for a second. What do you think was the problem with selling champagne to the captain of the *Titanic*?"

"It isn't what he really needed," I answered.

"And why is that a problem?" Marketing Mike asked.

"Because the *Titanic* sank, and they didn't have enough lifeboats and a lot of people died."

"That's right," Mike agreed. "And why is that bad for your business?"

"Because we lost a customer. The captain went down with the ship."

"You've got it. You see, most people don't care what they sell and who they sell it to. In fact, I believe most salespeople, in their own way, are simply selling champagne to the captain of the *Titanic*.

"And that's why their businesses falter and fail," he continued. "They aren't serving the true needs of their customers, and they aren't spending any time thinking about those needs. They're just trying to sell something—no matter what it is. And when their customer's ship goes down, they go down with it."

"So," I asked, "how do we establish long-term relationships with customers?"

"Start by looking at each situation through the eyes of the customer. Approach each prospect with no expectations or preconceived notions. Think about the customer's real problems. And try to spend the time needed to educate prospects about what you believe are their real issues."

"Just like the captain of the *Titanic*."

"That's right." Mike agreed. "Our lifeboat salesperson took the easy route. He didn't make the effort to convince the captain that his boat could sink. He went for the easy buck."

Marketing Mike's advice was another gem. Since that time, I've tried to approach every prospect with both an open mind and a helping attitude. As a result, I've helped more people and made more money.

SIX

The Box of Chocolate

My client Rudy was perplexed, frustrated, and worn out.

"I've been doing telemarketing for the past month," he complained. "I try to set up appointments with new prospects, but I keep running into a wall."

"Why, what's happening?" I asked.

"No one wants to speak with me. They hang up, or they don't call me back. No one wants to set up an appointment with me. It's really hard going."

I promised Rudy I would try to come up with a solution. Naturally, that meant that I would be speaking with Marketing Mike.

And, naturally, Marketing Mike got to the root of the problem.

"Most people would rather stick knitting needles in their eyes than meet with another salesperson," he explained.

"How come?"

"Because most salespeople come on too strong.

And they try to sell you something you don't really need."

"I guess that's why so many salespeople have a bad reputation, and why no one wants to meet with them," I commented. "But tell me, how do we sell things if no one wants to meet with a salesperson?"

"Well, it's a real problem," Marketing Mike said. "Most people will do almost anything to avoid another sales pitch."

"Like what?"

"People use all kinds of methods to block out salespeople and avoid sales pitches. They use call display to screen telemarketers. They use their TV remote to skip commercials. At work they use their secretaries to block salespeople. And they simply toss out flyers as junk mail."

"So you're saying that it's getting harder to reach prospects with a sales pitch?"

"That's right. In this day and age, people are overwhelmed by all the sales pitches coming their way. So they have put up barriers to keep them out. I call this 'The Sales-Pitch Bunker.'"

"I experience this problem in my own business," I said. "I get frustrated because I can't reach new prospects. They hang up on me. They don't return my calls, and they throw out my flyers without reading them."

"And what do you do when someone tries to sell you something?" Marketing Mike asked.

"I do the same thing. I hang up on them. I don't return their calls. And I throw out their flyers without reading them."

"Ironic, isn't it?"

"So," I asked, "if everyone is hiding behind their Sales-Pitch Bunker, how do we get new customers?"

"We have to get them to leave their bunker and come to us of their own free will," Marketing Mike said. "We have to play The Box of Chocolate marketing game."

"Okay," I said, hooked as always. "How does that work?"

Marketing Mike went on without missing a beat.

"Well, let's pretend you're trying to sell a box of chocolate. Most people try to sell their box of chocolate by holding up the box and describing the great chocolate inside. They explain how delicious they are, how fresh they are, and how many there are. Or they show a picture of the chocolate inside the box."

"What's wrong with that?" I asked.

"The problem is that most people will never even hear the story because they'll block it out. They don't want to hear another sales pitch. Or if they do listen, they may not believe all the claims made by the salesperson. And most important of all, it takes a lot of time and money to persuade people to buy a box of chocolate using only a sales pitch."

"So what should we do differently?"

"Think about it," Mike said. "What's a faster way to get people to buy a box of chocolate?"

"Give them a piece?"

"That's right. Give them a free sample. Let them experience the chocolate for themselves. Then they will want to buy the whole box."

"But won't it cost a lot of money to give away our product like that?"

"No. It's actually a lot faster and cheaper. You don't have to spend hours explaining your product and its features. You just let people taste. And you don't have to spend a fortune on advertising and other promotions. All you have to do is give them a taste."

"Is that how you get people to come out of their Sales-Pitch Bunker?" I asked. "Give them something for free?"

"That's right. In today's world, you have to give away free value to start relationships."

"But does this principle work in other kinds of businesses?" I asked.

"This marketing game works in every business," Marketing Mike continued. "If you are a consultant, give your prospects ninety minutes of free advice. If you are an accountant, give them a free audit of their books. If you are selling software, give them a free trial of your program. If you are a dentist, give them a free dental cleaning. Whatever your business is, think of something valuable that you can give away for free to get relationships started."

"What about discounts and coupons?" I asked. "Aren't those kinds of promotions free value?"

"No, they don't count because they're tied to a sale. You have to make a purchase to get the discount. If you want your free value to attract prospects, there can be no strings attached."

"But isn't there a risk that some people will take advantage of your generosity?"

"That will happen sometimes. But you'll get better at determining the people who qualify for your free value."

"Qualify?" I asked. "What do you mean by that?"

"Well, if you are going to give away free value, you are in a position to be selective about who will receive it. And by making the offer exclusive to certain types of people, more prospects will want it."

"And because it's not available to everyone, people will want it more," I added.

"That's right."

"Wow. I'm going to go back right now and help Rudy use The Box of Chocolate marketing game."

Over the next six months, Rudy's fortunes turned around. He developed a free workshop and wrote a free, informative book. When making sales calls, Rudy told his prospects that he had lots of free value to offer them. More and more prospects took Rudy up on his offer, and he started developing more relationships. These relationships naturally led to more sales.

In the years that followed, Marketing Mike's

advice helped me grow my business as well. As a marketing coach, I offer my prospects a free sixty-minute private workshop. During the workshop, I give them lots of free advice and plenty of great ideas. If I really like them, I give them free copies of my books. This approach attracts lots of prospects and generates lots of sales. And it was all because I listened to Marketing Mike, and I was willing to give away free value to start relationships.

So here's the challenge. Are you willing to offer free value? If so, what are you willing to do, or give, for free? Take the time to think about it. You'll be happily surprised with the results.

SEVEN

The Basketball Mind-Trap

Many years ago, while I was in high school during the '70s, I had a part-time job as a computer operator. I worked for a company that linked together more than 300 pharmacies to a mainframe computer. In those days, the computer filled a large room.

Late at night, I backed up the content of the computer's hard drive onto large tapes. These tapes were shipped off-site each morning to safeguard the data. It was a low-level job, but it sparked an interest in computer technology that has not abated to this day.

Fifteen years after this first foray into the world of computers, I found myself running a company that built and managed dozens of on-line networks using technology called Bulletin Board Systems, or BBS for short. In those days before the World Wide Web and the mass popularization of the Internet, I thought I had it all figured out. My business was growing so fast we couldn't keep up. Everyone, it seemed, was excited about what we had to offer.

Then one day, during our company's upward spiral to success, the World Wide Web appeared. Suddenly, no one was interested in Bulletin Board Systems. They wanted to talk about the World Wide Web. Our business went from boom to bust overnight. As someone quipped, we were "overnight failures."

Distraught, and not sure where to turn next, I sought out Marketing Mike for some words of wisdom.

"You had a great business going, but you were caught in The Basketball Mind-Trap," Mike said.

"What in the world is The Basketball Mind-Trap?" I asked him.

"That's when you build your business around a specific product or service and not around your customers."

"But we provided outstanding service to our customers," I said, defending myself.

"Of course you did. But that's not what I'm talking about."

I asked him to enlighten me.

"When you are caught in The Basketball Mind-Trap," Marketing Mike began, "all of your thinking starts with your product. In your case, all of your thinking started with your BBS systems. And when BBS systems were no longer popular, your business sank. Instead of thinking first about your customers, you were thinking first about your product.

You were being a salesperson, not a marketer."

"Okay," I agreed, "I think I see your point. But what's this business about basketballs?"

"It's a story I tell to explain the problem. Let's pretend there's a company called Bouncy Basketballs. Of course, they make basketballs. They have been in business for a long time, and they've made a lot of money. But something has gone wrong. Their sales have fallen. The basketball industry has become much more competitive. Margins are slim, the company has laid off people, and there are a lot of long faces in the boardroom. The really sad part is that they can't figure out how to turn things around."

"Why not?"

"Because they are caught in The Basketball Mind-Trap. They have been selling basketballs for so long, they can't think about anything else. They have run out of creative ideas because all their thinking starts and ends with basketballs."

"And they're not thinking about their customers," I chimed in.

"That's right. Their customers are an afterthought. Sure, the company provides good service. They have a newsletter. They take their distributors out to play golf. But it won't help them get out of their predicament, because they still think they are in the business of making and selling basketballs."

"So what business are they really in?" I asked.

"They are in the business of helping their customers. And to escape from their mind-trap, they need to start all their thinking with their customers."

"So how do you do that?"

"You begin by picking a specific customer type. In this case, who do you think is their customer type?"

"Well, I assume their customers are basketball players."

"That's right. Basketball players."

"So how is that helpful?"

"It changes everything. If they start all their thinking with basketball players, they will begin to see the way out of their problem."

"How so?"

"They'll start thinking of new ways to help basketball players and to develop long-term, profitable relationships with them. For example, they could develop software to help coaches organize basketball teams. They could build basketball courts and sell basketball uniforms. They could also develop a Web site that offers basketball books, videos, on-line chat rooms, and other features."

"But," I wondered aloud, "maybe they don't know how to do those things."

"That's probably true. So either they learn how or they partner with other companies that can do those things. It doesn't really matter. Bouncy Basketballs can't go wrong if their goal is to develop strong, lasting relationships with millions of basketball players."

"But won't that take a long time?"

"Developing relationships takes time," Marketing Mike agreed, "but what's the alternative? If they keep trying to push their basketballs, they'll probably go out of business, or they'll suffer a long, painful decline. But if they turn their thinking around, they may start coming up with new ideas on how to get more customers, how to make more money, and how to grow their business."

"Let me make sure I understand you," I said. "You're saying that Bouncy Basketballs hit a wall because they thought that they were in only the basketball business."

"That's correct."

"And the way forward is for them to turn their thinking around: to see their business as a company that helps basketball players succeed and enjoy the sport more."

"Right again."

"And if they build their business around basketball players, their thinking and creativity will be greatly expanded. They'll now be able to give themselves permission to help basketball players in any way possible."

"You've got the idea," Marketing Mike said, waiting for my next comment.

"And you're also saying that this problem is all in our minds."

"That's why I call it a 'mind-trap.' Most of the time, the things holding us back are ideas and beliefs we cling to in our minds. To change, we have to change the way we think."

"Okay," I then asked, "so how do I escape from The Basketball Mind-Trap and grow my business?"

"Well, it's really easy. Who do you like working with most?"

"I like working with business owners."

"So I recommend that you make business owners your customer type."

"That's good."

"Now, what are the three things you think business owners want most of all?"

"They want to get more customers, they want to make more money, and they want to grow their business."

"So how could you help them do all of that?"

"I could do consulting," I began. "I could write books. I could give speeches. I could create software programs. I could build Web sites. I could do a lot of things."

"Now you're getting the idea. You could do hundreds of things."

"But I can't do all of those things at once."

"No, but you can start somewhere. And then you can add value components as you go along."

"What are value components?"

"They're additional products and services." Marketing Mike informed me. "But the term 'value components' indicates that they can be mixed and matched to suit the individual needs of each customer."

"Okay," I summed up, "I'll keep working on developing my value components, but my main focus will be on helping business owners become more successful."

"That will make all the difference in the world."

As usual, Marketing Mike was right. In building my business around business owners, I became more creative and enthusiastic. This approach also gave me a clear direction for our business. Since that day, I have worked with thousands of business owners. I've written books, given speeches, held workshops, and developed software. And no matter what happens in the future, I know I will always be able to help business owners. This book is an example of that philosophy.

So why don't you think about your situation. Are you caught in The Basketball Mind-Trap? Do you start your thinking with your products and services, or with your customers? Decide who your favourite customers are and make them your number-one customer type. Think of new value components that you can offer them.

It might make all the difference in the world.

EIGHT

The Birdcage Brochure

During my first meeting with a new consulting client, the president of the company said, "We have a problem with our marketing. We created this brochure for our trade show last year. Now we have about 10 000 brochures left over, and we don't know what to do with them. Can you help us figure out a way to use them?"

The question took me aback, so I asked some questions of my own. "What do you use the brochure for now? Do you give it out to prospects?"

"Well, we haven't been using it at all."

"How come?"

"Because it's pretty out of date."

"What do you mean?"

"Well, we don't sell some of these products and services anymore. And some of the people in the team picture don't work here anymore. And we changed our Web site address too."

"So, you're telling me that your brochures are out of date," I responded, "but you would still like to use them for something. Is that right?"

"That's it. We spent a lot of money on them, and it seems a waste just to throw them out."

I said I would think about their dilemma and get back to them. Once again, I sought out Marketing Mike.

"They've got a Birdcage Brochure on their hands," Marketing Mike said.

"What's a Birdcage Brochure?"

"I call it that because the only thing you can use it for is to line a birdcage. That brochure is now completely useless."

"You think so?"

"It's a common problem. They built a brochure for a specific event—a trade show—and now they're stuck with a bunch of them after the event is over. So they wasted a lot of money."

"What should they do differently in the future?"

"Well, instead of focusing on a particular marketing tool—a brochure, advertising, or a direct-mail piece—you need to start by developing your marketing blueprint first."

"Why would that work better?"

"It helps you avoid getting stuck with a Birdcage Brochure for one thing. And you might figure out that you didn't need a brochure at all. You could discover that there's a better way to get more customers and make more money."

"So you're saying that you need to develop a marketing strategy first, and then build the tools if you need them."

"It's kind of like building a house. You wouldn't build a house without having an architect design it first, would you?"

"That would be pretty stupid."

"That's right. But many people create expensive marketing tools without first designing a marketing blueprint. And sometimes marketing tools can cost a lot more than a house."

"That makes sense," I said. "So how do you create a marketing blueprint?"

"Well, there are a number of key steps," Marketing Mike said, rolling up his sleeves. "First off, you have to choose your customer type."

"Yes, I remember that. You need to decide which type of customer you want to reach."

"It's really important that you choose just one customer type at a time to focus on," Marketing Mike emphasized. "If you don't, you may go off in too many different directions. You need to focus your limited marketing time and money on your most important customer type."

"So you need to decide if you want to focus on dog catchers, nurses, professional bridge players, or some other specific type of person," I said.

"You've got it," Marketing Mike said enthusiastically. "Choosing your customer type is your most important decision. So make your choice carefully."

"Then what do you do?"

"Then you determine if you are selling the right products and services. Often people are creating brochures for products and services that no one wants. In some cases, it's not the brochure that isn't working. You're just not selling the right things."

"So how do you know if you're selling the right products or services?"

"That can be a complicated proposition, but you've already simplified the matter. When you are focusing on a specific customer, it's easier to come up with new ways to help. In most cases, you just have to come up with something new that no one else is selling."

"How will that work?"

"Well, let's pretend that we own a bowling alley. Up until now, we have focused on selling bowling time. But that's a commodity. Every bowling alley sells time on their lanes."

"So what could we do differently?"

"You could sell themed bowling parties with special guests like celebrities and sports figures. You could videotape people bowling. You could have a Web site where people can post their scores and arrange matches with other people. You could have contests with prizes provided by local sponsors. You could put in a daycare centre so new parents can do some bowling. There is really no end to the possible ideas."

"So you're saying that people are interested in new things."

"That's right. If you are going to promote your business, you've got to have something new to say, or no one will listen. Most brochures are boring because there's nothing new or exciting in them."

"Okay," I asked, "so what's the third step?"

"Now you have to decide what you're willing to give away for free in order to start new relationships."

"I remember that one," I said proudly. "That's the story about The Box of Chocolate. You have to give people some value for free so that people will come out of their Sales-Pitch Bunker."

"You have learned your lessons well, young Skywalker," Marketing Mike joked. "In the case of our bowling alley, you could give away a free picture of the customer bowling. The free offer will also add some spark to our marketing tools."

"So we've got our customer type. We've got some new products and services to sell. And we've got some free value to offer. What's next?"

"Then you lay out your marketing process. You figure out the steps you will use to attract your customers and get them to buy your products and services."

"How does that work?"

"Well, the first step is always the same: Make the customer become aware of you. This is the most important step, and the point at which you will focus most marketing time and money. For example, to make the customer aware of your bowling alley and its special promotions, you might do a few things: advertise in the local paper, post flyers around the community, or send out a direct mail piece. You could also provide an incentive for your regular customers to bring in a friend."

"What kind of incentive?"

"You could give your customers free bowling time for every new friend they bring into the bowling alley. Or they could get special prizes."

"Why is it important to work through the steps of your marketing process?"

"Because it will tell you exactly what marketing tools you need. In the case of our bowling alley, we may discover that we don't need a brochure but that we do need advertising, a flyer, and a Web site. And most importantly, we won't end up with a Birdcage Brochure."

"That sounds great," I said, thanking Marketing Mike once again for his wise counsel. "I'll start putting these ideas into place right away."

The next day, I visited my clients and informed them that they were stuck with a Birdcage Brochure. After they recovered from their initial disappointment, and because they did not own a bird of any description, they ceremoniously hauled the many boxes of their Birdcage Brochure into the trash. Then we settled down to the task of developing their marketing blueprint and building more appropriate marketing tools. And, once again, I discovered that Marketing Mike was right. By working through the process he suggested, they ended up getting more customers and making more money.

So the question is this: Do you have a Birdcage Brochure on your hands? (Or perhaps, you're creating one.) Stop for a second and think about it. Developing a marketing blueprint first may save you a lot of time and money.

NINE

The Big Idea

Over the years, I've worked with many different kinds of companies. But only one was involved with the toilet industry.

"I'm in the toilet business, and I'm proud of it," my client Maurice exclaimed without a hint of irony or sarcasm. "We are an essential service because everyone needs toilets."

Technically speaking, Maurice wasn't actually in toilets. His company sold equipment to keep washrooms in restaurants and other public places sanitary and smelling fresh.

"We have a great business," Maurice continued. "But we have a big problem. Even though lots of companies need our products and services, most people don't want to talk about toilets. So it's hard to meet new prospects."

"What have you tried so far?" I asked. "Have you tried advertising, direct mail, or public relations?"

"Well, we attended a big restaurant convention last year," Maurice told me, "but we didn't get visitors to our booth. We spent a lot of money with little to show for it. Now we're scheduled to attend the same convention in three weeks, and we don't want to waste our time again."

"What did you do with your booth last year?" I asked, interested in knowing how a company involved in sanitation would equip a trade show booth.

"We had a few toilets and urinals on display, plus some brochures and some refreshments," he answered.

Sensing immediately that Maurice had a problem seeing things from the customer's perspective, I made an observation.

"Maybe people don't want to hang out in a booth with a bunch of urinals," I proffered gingerly. "And maybe the idea of having refreshments while standing beside a toilet is a bit surreal for some people."

"We thought that might be a problem, but we didn't know what else to do with our booth. After all, our business is about toilets. Can you think of something we can do to make our booth more exciting this year?"

Not having worked on a toilet-related marketing program before, I told Maurice that I would put my mind to it and get back to him.

Luckily, Marketing Mike had some time available, so I gave him the scoop on Maurice and his dilemma.

"You need to do something exciting and interesting that is going to get people into the booth," Mike said. "You need The Big Idea."

"What do you mean by The Big Idea?"

"The Big Idea is a concept that will get people's attention. It can be a contest, a new product, a special program, or something really wacky. Your client Maurice really needs a big idea, because if he just sits there with his toilets and urinals I don't think he is going to get a lot of visitors. Let's face it. You don't need to visit a booth to look at toilets. You just have to go to the bathroom."

"So what is The Big Idea that will get people to visit a booth displaying toilets and urinals?"

"Well, let's put our heads together," Mike said. And over the next hour we came up with what we thought was a brilliant strategy.

A few days later, I met with Maurice and presented the plan. "We need to stage a contest to drive people into your booth," I said, starting off slowly.

"What kind of contest?" Maurice asked.

"It is a contest to win a weekend in Niagara Falls. We thought the falling, flushing water of the falls would conjure up the right image about your products and services."

"So how does that help us get more people into our booth?"

"Well, we're going to hand out cards at various points around the convention. The cards will have invisible ink indicating if you've won a prize. But you have to bring the card to the booth and put it under an ultraviolet light to see if it's a winner."

Maurice loved the idea, and over the next few weeks we put the contest together. We hired two attractive models to hand out the cards. At the show, the models wore white lab coats and handed out the cards to convention delegates.

Within the first hour of the show, Maurice and his team had a long lineup waiting to get into his booth. The lineup attracted even more attention from passersby who joined the crowd to get in on the action. Over the three-day period more than 3000 people visited Maurice's booth. He met hundreds of prospects and set up a year's worth of appointments, which ultimately generated millions in additional revenues.

"It was such a simple idea, but it worked great," I told Marketing Mike. "Why don't more people put on promotions like that?"

"Most people take a really boring approach to these things," Mike said. "They don't add any sizzle or fun to the proceedings. They just hang up a shingle and wait for people to come to them. In other words, they neglect to develop The Big Idea."

"I think some people are just afraid to try new things," I added. "I think they're terrified that the idea just won't work."

"Well, it doesn't really matter if the first idea works," Mike continued. "If it works, that's terrific. But if it doesn't work, then at least you've learned something. As I said, marketing is about experimenting and trying new things. Sooner or later, you figure out what works."

Over the following years, the success of

Maurice's Niagara Falls contest led to a series of other big ideas for other clients, including The "Miss Bikini Shaver" Contest (because of budget constraints, I was obliged to act as my own one-man judge), The Adult Diaper Awareness Campaign, and my award-winning campaign promoting The Singing Clowns Jug Band (not a high point in my career, according to my wife).

So if you are embarking on a new campaign to promote your business, start by asking yourself, "What's our Big Idea?"

And remember, no matter what you come up with, try to have some fun with it.

TEN

The $5 Cup of Coffee

Borden Bond, president and founder of Gleaming Lake Cement Company, was expressing his exasperation over the falling price of cement.

"Every day, the global price for cement keeps falling," Borden lamented. "The market is flooded with cement so our profits are shrinking. If this keeps up, we'll need to lay off people and start closing some of our plants."

"That's terrible," I said. "What's the price for cement right now? How much does it cost per bag?"

"Today's price is $3.50 a bag wholesale," Borden said. "That's down from $3.85 last week and $4.18 last month."

"What's the average price?" I asked.

"Around $4.00 a bag. That's been the average price for the past five years."

I could tell from our discussion that Borden Bond and his company were mired in a commodity trap.

"Have you ever thought about developing something new, something that you could do to make more money and break out of your commodity business?"

"We've spent hours thinking about the problem and trying to come up with new ideas, but we haven't come up with anything."

"Why do you think you've failed to come up with an idea?" I asked.

"I don't know. It's just this business. Nobody is going to pay more than $4.00 for a bag of cement. That's the standard price, and I guess we're just stuck with it."

I told Borden that I would dwell on his dilemma and get back to him with some new ideas. Of course, that meant another rendezvous at the coffee shop with the venerable Marketing Mike.

"This is a classic case," Marketing Mike said, as he sipped his no-fat, extra-hot, skim milk vanilla latte. "Borden Bond and his team are stuck in concrete incremental thinking."

"What does that mean?" I asked, gulping down my extra-large, organic, fair trade, shade-grown Columbia espresso.

"It's like their mind is caught inside a prison. They can't think of anything new to do for their customers because they don't think that anyone will spend more than $4.00 for a bag of cement."

"But why are they so stuck?" I said, biting into my fresh baked, extra large carrot cake.

"Because they look at their industry and think that $4.00 cement is what it's all about. So they get stuck, and are unable to think big."

"So what can Borden do to increase his profits, think bigger, and break out of his commodity trap?" I asked.

"He has to use The Packaging Principle," Marketing Mike said, as he eased back into a comfortable, capacious leather chair located in front of the store's roaring fireplace.

"What's The Packaging Principle?"

"It is a creative method you can use to come up with new ideas, think bigger, and make a lot more money."

"So tell me more; how does it work?"

"Since we are enjoying ourselves in their establishment, let's use Starbucks as our example. In the early 1990s, the people at Starbucks had a vision. They had a vision of a coffee cup with $5.00 written on it."

"Why?" I asked.

"They wanted to figure out a way that they could get people to pay $5.00 for a cup of coffee."

"Just like we did today when we bought our coffee," I added.

"That's right. But back in the early 1990s, other people in the industry thought the vision was ludicrous. After all, at that time the average cost for a cup of coffee was 50 cents. It was unimaginable that someone would pay $5.00. Maybe 60 cents, but certainly not $5.00."

"So how did they pull it off?" I queried. "How

did they get us to pay $5.00?"

"They used The Packaging Principle."

"How does that work?"

"You start by taking a box, either real or imagined, and put a really big price on it. In this case, they used a coffee cup and put $5.00 on it. It is the same as using a box."

"How is that helpful?"

"Once you have the box, and a big price on it, you start to think of things that you can put into the box that will justify the price to customers. This process opens up your mind, and forces you to think bigger. It breaks you out of your incremental mindset."

"I get that. But what did Starbucks do?"

"They packaged their business differently from the competition. To get people to pay $5.00 for a cup of coffee, they realized that they had to create a completely different kind of experience. Something better. Something way beyond the ordinary."

"So what kinds of things did they do?"

"To justify the $5.00 price tag, they created a wonderful environment with beautiful décor, leather couches, and a blazing fireplace. They also served dozens of different high-quality coffees that you can get made to order in just a few minutes. So now people are lining up to pay $5.00, and they love it. It is worth every penny in the mind of the customer."

"But doesn't coffee cost just pennies a pound? Why do customers gladly pay $5.00?"

"Because they are paying for the experience, not the coffee. Remember, the real value is not your product or service, it is the value that the customer perceives in his or her mind. If the customer thinks it is worth $5.00, then it is worth $5.00."

"That's fascinating," I said. "So how can we use The Packaging Principle to help Borden Bond and his cement company?"

"Here's what you do," Mike said, laying out in detail how to apply The Packaging Principle.

The next week, I was back at the company's head office, with a box in hand, to work with Borden and his marketing team.

"We are going to start by leaving your $4.00 bags of cement outside this room for the next three hours. Is that okay?" I asked.

"We'll give it a try," Borden promised.

"All right. Now let's take this box and put a number on it. If you could create something new and sell it for a lot of money, what dollar figure would get you really excited?"

"Well, how about $10 000?" Borden suggested. "It sounds ridiculous, but I'll play along with the game."

"Nobody in our industry is going to pay $10 000 for anything. They pay $4.00 a bag and that's it," one of the team members blurted out.

The other people on Borden's team also expressed their skepticism, but agreed to keep going anyway.

"Well, let's see what happens," I said. "What

could we put into the box that would justify charging your customers $10 000?"

"We could develop a cement product that dries faster and lasts longer," someone suggested.

"Okay. Write that down on a piece of paper and put it in the box. What else could you do?"

"We could develop diagnostic equipment that monitors the elasticity and durability of the cement."

"We could provide a software program that helps design the most efficient cement and aggregate mixtures for each project."

"We could offer courses to teach people how to build new things with cement."

"We could develop new mixing equipment that is computerized and self-cleaning."

For the next three hours, the team came up with one idea after another. Some of the ideas were simple, some were outrageous, and some were absolutely brilliant.

"I can't believe all of the great ideas we came up with," Borden said at the end of the session. "I can see dozens of ways that we can make more money and break out of our commodity trap."

And so he did. Over the next three years, the company changed its name to Gleaming Lake Enterprises and completely transformed the concrete industry. Their new products and innovations, packaged in original ways, convinced thousands of customers to spend $10 000 with the company.

To fully appreciate the power of The Packaging

Principle, I had a debriefing session with Marketing Mike.

"Why does this principle work so well?" I asked. "Why does it get people thinking so creatively?"

"Most of us get caught up in incremental thinking because we can't see beyond the boundaries of our existing industry. The other coffee companies were stuck with their 50-cent cups of coffee because they were just thinking about the coffee, and what everyone else was charging for it. There was no room in their minds for new ideas or for thinking big.

"But when you put a big price on a box, it gives you permission to think big. You have to start filling the box with new ideas. And because it is just a game, you don't have to worry about how you are going to make it happen. So you feel free to be creative."

"That's why Starbucks is so successful," I added. "By packaging their business around their vision of a $5.00 cup of coffee, they made that vision a reality."

"That's right," Marketing Mike said. "If you want to break out of your commodity business, you have to start with a vision of something bigger. Then you figure out how to make it happen."

ELEVEN

The Gourmet Meal

Tiny's Books was my favourite bookstore. A bear of a man, Tiny had been running the store in my neighbourhood for more than fifteen years. He had a vast knowledge of books and literature, and was a great storyteller. Unfortunately, Tiny had a big problem.

"These big-box bookstores are killing me," Tiny moaned. "They're driving down the prices of books. I just can't compete with them."

"Do people really want to drive out to the suburbs to save a few dollars on books?" I asked Tiny.

"Enough people to take a big bite out of my profits," he said. "In fact, if things continue like this, I'll be out of business in six months."

Worried that my favourite bookstore would disappear, I promised Tiny I would think about his problem and try to come up with a viable solution. I told him I would seek out my trusty mentor, Marketing Mike.

"This is a classic case of Fast Food versus The Gourmet Meal," Mike explained after I had told him about Tiny's dilemma.

"What's that?" I asked him.

"All business in the future will fall into one of two categories: Fast Food or The Gourmet Meal," Mike went on. "The fast-food companies will focus on the mass market. They will have lots of customers and they will compete on price. In order to survive, they will have to be extremely efficient. They'll have to use things like call centres, bank machines, and drive-through windows to serve their customers."

"The Gourmet Meal companies will focus on a small number of high-quality customers. They'll offer high-end products and services."

"So how does this relate to Tiny's problem?" I asked.

"Well, the big bookstores are selling fast food—fast-food books. They have millions of customers and they compete on price. No matter what Tiny does, he won't be able to beat the big bookstores at the fast-food game. He doesn't have the resources."

"So what should he do?"

"Tiny needs to take a completely different tack. He needs to offer a gourmet meal instead."

"What do you mean by that?"

"Tiny needs to develop something new that caters to the individual needs and wishes of his best customers. He has to provide things that the big stores can't."

"Like what?"

"There are lots of things he can do," Mike continued. "For example, he can get to know the reading interests of his customers and store them in a database. Then he could become much more proactive by calling them to suggest new books. He could host book clubs, and have authors give readings at his store. He could link up with the local university and offer discounts on literature courses. He could create a customized electronic newsletter that sends you information about upcoming books by your favourite authors. He could set up a dating service for people who love to read. He could develop a Web site that helps people sell and exchange rare books."

"Wow," I enthused. "You have lots of ideas. But how is he going to do all that?"

"Well, I'm not suggesting he do all these things at once. I'm just using them as examples to show that there are many ways to create a gourmet meal."

"Do you have any other ideas?"

"Absolutely. Tiny could specialize in a particular type of audience. He could run a bookstore for teachers, or lawyers, or teenagers. He could focus on a particular type of book, such as mysteries, or romance, or historical biographies."

"How would specializing help Tiny?"

"If he specializes in a particular market or type of book, he will become an expert in that area. People will seek him out because they can't get that kind of specialized knowledge from a clerk at the big bookstores."

"You're right. The big stores have so many different books that no one there can be an expert in all of them."

"And," Marketing Mike went on, "if Tiny were to become an expert in a particular subject, such as travel books, he could branch out into all kinds of things related to travel. He could start selling travel videos, or even start a travel agency. There are so many things he could do to turn his business into a gourmet meal."

"So let me get this straight," I said. "You can run either a fast-food business or a gourmet-meal business. The fast-food companies are usually really big with lots of customers, and they compete on price. The gourmet-meal companies focus on a small select group of high-quality customers by offering something extraordinary that isn't available anywhere else."

"That's right."

"Is there anything in between fast food and a gourmet meal?"

"Nothing but misery," Marketing Mike replied.

"Why is that?" I asked.

"Let me tell you a story," Marketing Mike began. "There was a restaurant that got caught between fast food and the gourmet meal. The owner was a fantastic chef. His meals were superb. But his restaurant looked like a cheap diner. The meals on his menu cost more than fast-food places in the neigh-bourhood, but were less expensive than the fancy restaurants.

"When people walked by his establishment, they looked in the window and saw what they thought was a fast-food restaurant. Then they looked at the menu and saw the high prices. So they wondered: Is this an expensive fast-food restaurant or a cheap gourmet restaurant? Unable to decide, they moved on. And that's why hardly anyone ate at this restau-rant and why the owner went out of business. It wasn't one or the other."

"So you're saying that you have to decide which type of business you are in."

"That's right. You are either fast food or a gourmet meal. Neither one is better than the other. You just have to decide which one you are and stick to it."

"But can't you offer a gourmet meal at lower prices?" I wondered.

"You could, but no one would believe you."

"Why?"

"Because people know that you can't get a gour-met meal on the cheap. If you don't charge a lot for a gourmet meal, you can't provide the special ingre-dients, the high-quality service, and the ambience. It's just fake gourmet. And everyone can see through that charade."

Intrigued by this concept, I returned to Tiny's Books brimming with many ideas on how Tiny could transform his business.

Initially, Tiny resisted them all.

"These things sound risky," he said.

"Well, you've got to do something or you'll be broke in six months."

"You've got that right."

"So are you willing to try and turn your business into a gourmet meal?"

"Sure, why not?" he eventually agreed.

Over the next six months, Tiny and I worked hard to transform his business. We built a database with lots of information about his very best customers. We created an electronic newsletter that distributed personalized messages to each customer. We created a book club. We held special events, and started adult literacy programs taught by local school teachers. We built a Web site specializing in books about hiking (one of Tiny's favourite topics). And Tiny made an effort to get to know his customers better.

Soon after the start-up period, Tiny noticed that his sales were going up. He stopped thinking about the big bookstores across town. He also stopped worrying about his prices. In fact, he raised them by ten percent.

Most important, Tiny started to realize that he had lots of things to offer that the big bookstores could never provide. He began to look at himself as a gourmet chef of books.

So take a hard look at your business and your industry. What type of business do you want to be in: fast food or gourmet meal? This decision may be the most important one you ever make in your business.

TWELVE

Opening Their Wallets

"We've spent a lot of time and money on these seminars, but we're not getting enough new clients!" Nelda Blyss barked, as she stomped around her boardroom. "We must be doing something wrong."

"What are the seminars for?" I asked her. "What are you selling?"

"We have these seminars to promote our Hospital Profit Program. We coach hospital administrators on how to run their operations more profitably."

"Are you getting a lot of people to come to your seminars?"

"They're jammed," Nelda boasted. "All of these administrators are under pressure to become more profitable, and they are just starved for information."

"That's great. So what's the problem?" I asked. "It sounds like a big success."

"The seminars are fine. But we are not getting enough people to sign up for our Hospital Profit Program. They express a lot of interest, but when we follow up the next week, we can't get them to sign on."

"How much do you charge for the seminar and how much for your program?"

"We offer the seminar for free, and we charge $5000 to participate in our program for one year."

"Is the program successful? Do the people in the program like it?"

"Once we get people in the program, they love it," Nelda said. "That's not our problem. We are just not converting enough people from the seminar into members of our program. There is something missing."

I told Nelda that I would consult with my marketing mentor and get back to her with some kind of idea to solve her problem.

The next day, Marketing Mike listened to Nelda's predicament, and offered these words of sage advice.

"Nelda needs to add a few more elements to her marketing process," he said. "Right now, she is having a hard time getting people to open their wallets even though they are very interested in her program."

"So why do you think that her prospects are not willing to open their wallets?" I asked.

"Well, it's like she's walking leisurely along a long flat beach with her prospect, and they are having a nice chat. Then they arrive at this vertical cliff that is 5000 feet high, and she asks them if they would like to climb it. And most of them say no."

"How come?"

"Because it is too big a change. One minute they are walking along a flat beach, and then suddenly they have to climb this huge cliff."

"Okay. I understand the story, but how does it relate to Nelda's situation?"

"The seminar is the beach. It's free, so it isn't hard for people to participate in. And her program is the cliff. It's $5000, which seems pretty steep for someone who has been walking along a free, flat beach."

"Are you saying that she should charge less for her program?"

"No, not at all. I'm saying that she needs to get them to open their wallets for something else before she asks them for the $5000."

"Why is that?"

"If you can get prospects to open up their wallets and give you money, even for a small amount like $50, they will be more likely to keep giving you money, even if the next request is for $5000."

"That's incredible. How does that work?"

"The first big step in a business relationship is to convert someone from a prospect into a customer. When someone is a prospect, they haven't made any commitment, or invested anything but time in their relationship with you. They are still shopping around.

"But when they open their wallets and give you some money, their whole perception of the relationship has changed. They see themselves as a customer. They have made a commitment and they have made an investment, no matter how small it may be."

"So the trick is to get them to buy something for a small amount so they will be more open to spending a larger amount later."

"You've got it. The key thing to remember is: If you can get prospects to open their wallets once, they are more likely to keep opening their wallets, for larger and larger amounts."

"That's great," I said. "So how do we get Nelda's prospects to open their wallets?"

Over the next half an hour, Marketing Mike and I cooked up a strategy that applied the Open Wallet Concept, and even took the idea to a higher level of sophistication.

The next day, I met with Nelda and explained our recommendations. She was interested, but also incredulous.

"I really don't think this is going to work, but I'll give it a try," she said.

Two weeks later, Nelda stood in front of fifty hospital managers and administrators and said, "Thank for attending our seminar. Before we get started, I want to make you aware of a special offer we have for you today. The next step after our seminar is a 90-minute coaching session that is normally priced at $300. However, we are willing to give you this coaching session for free, if you purchase our Hospital Profit Starter Kit today for $50. The kit contains our book, three valuable research papers, and ten passes for our on-line staff assessment survey, valued at more than $200."

The next day, I phoned Nelda to see what had happened. "It's unbelievable," she said. "We sold twenty-two starter kits. That money paid for the costs of the seminar. We also signed up all twenty-two of them for their coaching sessions."

I congratulated Nelda and told her to call me after she had completed most of the coaching sessions.

A few weeks later I asked, "So what happened after the coaching sessions? Did more people sign up?"

"I don't know why, but sixteen people signed up for the program and paid their $5 000 up front. Whatever is going on worked great."

I called Marketing Mike immediately to get an explanation for why Nelda's new approach was working so beautifully.

"It is all about opening their wallets," Marketing Mike said. "At the seminar, the people bought the $50 package because they wanted to get the valuable ingredients and save $300 on the coaching session."

"So they paid the $50 because they could get the package and a free $300 session?"

"That's right. Because they had opened their

wallets and paid the $50, they were now in a trans-actional relationship with Nelda and her company. In other words, they were now in the habit of giving money to Nelda, so their relationship changed fundamentally."

"I understand all of that, but tell me more."

"The next thing that happened was that everyone showed up for their coaching session because they had invested $50 and didn't want to waste it. As a result, Nelda didn't have to track them down or put up with no-shows."

"But why did so many people sign up for the program? Five thousand dollars is a lot of money."

"They signed up for the program because they had worked through the coaching session, but, more importantly, they signed up because they didn't want to waste their original $50 investment."

"You mean they opened their wallets for $5000 because they didn't want to waste $50. That sounds crazy."

"But that's how human beings behave. If they have made an investment of time and money in something, they are more inclined to keep going. Otherwise, they feel that they have wasted their time and are not acting consistently."

"What do you mean 'consistently'?"

"Once people have started to behave in a certain way, they want to keep behaving that way in order to reinforce their self-image as a consistent person. It is a fundamental aspect of human nature. That's why it is so important to get your prospects to open their wallets as soon as possible."

At that, I simply stared at Marketing Mike, my mind exploding with possibilities.

THIRTEEN

The Quick-Fix Pill

Lucan Wade, a financial adviser with The Zodiac Financial Group, was frustrated, and he didn't mind expressing it.

"I just met with a wonderful couple, but I couldn't get them to work with me. They wanted to buy some disability insurance, but they said they could get it somewhere else for less money. I couldn't get them to see that I could help them in so many other ways."

"Does that happen a lot?" I asked. "Do a lot of your prospects fail to appreciate all of the added value that you have to offer?"

"More than I would like to think about," Lucan admitted. "I know that there are a lot of people who just want to buy something quick and cheap, but I also know that there are many other prospects who need a lot more help. The trick is getting them to understand that, and I don't know how."

I told Lucan that I would sleep on his issue and get back to him with some nuggets of wisdom. Next stop: Marketing Mike.

"Lucan's problem is universal," Marketing Mike said. "Most people want to believe that all of their problems can be solved quickly and easily. That's why people fall for quick weight-loss diets and instant beauty aids. They don't want to do the work required to get real, lasting results, so they fall for the quick-fix solution."

"That's kind of sad."

"It's just human nature. We all do it. We all want to hope that our problems can be solved quickly, easily, and for little money."

"So how do we sell people what really works?" I asked. "Especially when the solution requires an investment on their part of more time, energy, and money?"

"Well, imagine you're a doctor, and a patient shows up with a headache. The patient hopes that it is just a headache and asks for a quick-fix pill. Naturally, he wants to solve his problem with a quick-fix pill. Who wouldn't?"

"But as a doctor, you know that the problem could be much worse. Some of your patients with the same symptoms were diagnosed with a brain tumour. So you tell the patient that he might have a more serious problem and needs to go through some tests."

"That sounds like a good idea," I said.

"It is a good idea, but the patient is resistant. He doesn't want to hear that he might have a brain tumour. He just wants to get his pill and get going.

He doesn't want to go through a long, involved process."

"But he might die if he doesn't."

"I know. But the news comes as a shock, and he blames it on the doctor. Kind of like shooting the messenger."

"So what do you do? How can you get the patient or prospect to address the bigger problem?" I asked.

"In Lucan's case, it is even harder. If a doctor tells you that your headache might be a brain tumour, you will probably listen eventually. But when a financial adviser tells you that you need to develop a detailed financial plan or you will go broke, you might just ignore that advice, and put your head in the sand like an ostrich."

"So what can Lucan do?"

"He needs to start by explaining the problem in more detail. He needs to explain that people who buy financial tools by searching for the lowest price often end up with the wrong tools and actually end up paying too much."

"What's the best way for him to explain the problem?"

"He can give the problem a name. For example, he might call it 'The Tools-Only Trap.'"

"Why is naming the problem so helpful?" I asked.

"Naming the problem makes it easier for the prospect to understand and remember it. It also gives him greater focus. That's why it is so important for doctors to identify and name a disease.

Then everyone can get focused on finding a cure."

"So you're saying that we should help our prospects understand the problem first before we present the solution."

"That's right. If we simply explain our full-blown solution, it won't make any sense to people who are just looking for the quick-fix pill. They won't understand what it has to do with them, and they won't buy it."

"Okay, so we've named the problem, and we've explained it. In Lucan's case, he explains The Tools-Only Trap and why that's a big problem. What does he do next?"

"The next step is for the prospects to diagnose themselves. They have to come to the conclusion on their own that they might have this big problem."

"So you're saying that we can't convince them on our own. Is that right?"

"That's right. No matter what you say, they won't really believe it. They will just think you are trying to sell them something expensive that they don't need."

"So what do we do?"

"I recommend that you create a scorecard that they can fill out. Get them to do a self-assessment questionnaire. Then ask them questions that will get them to admit their problems, and what they are going to do to fix those problems."

"Why does that work?"

"It works because the prospects go through their

own guided-thinking process that leads them to the conclusion that they need more than just a quick-fix pill."

"I can see how that would work. But why is all of this extra work necessary? I would think that most of Lucan's prospects are quite bright and can understand things pretty quickly."

"That's true to some degree. Most of Lucan's prospects are professionals with university educations. Unfortunately, when it comes to financial planning, they are still in Grade Two."

"What do you mean, Grade Two?"

"No matter what you are selling, most of your prospects are in Grade Two with regards to your industry and your business. They might be Einsteins in their own industries, but when it comes to your business, they don't know anything."

"Why is that a problem?"

"It's a huge problem because we assume that they understand what we're talking about. We make our presentation, and they nod politely at the right time even if they don't have a clue. They don't ask questions because they don't want to look stupid, or they are just being polite. But because they are in Grade Two, they don't have enough knowledge to buy your university-level solution. Somehow, you have to get them to Grade Twelve before they will be ready to buy."

"How do you get them to Grade Twelve?" I asked.

"Naming the problem and putting them through a self-diagnosis is very useful in this regard. You also need to engage in Educational Marketing."

"What is Educational Marketing?"

"That's when you make an effort to educate your prospects about the concepts related to your business."

"Does that mean that Lucan should educate his prospects about stocks and bonds?"

"Not at all. That would be boring. But he should educate his clients about why it is ineffective to buy financial products without having a financial plan first. If Lucan teaches his prospects this key concept, they will be more likely to buy his advanced solutions."

Over the next six months, I helped Lucan develop his educational marketing campaign. He wrote an article about The Tools-Only Trap, and gave speeches and seminars. He also created an educational package with an audio CD presentation about the value of financial planning. In addition, Lucan put his prospects through a self-assessment during his first meeting with them.

These tools and activities made a big difference for Lucan and his team. He got more attention by presenting himself as an educator, not just another adviser trying to sell something. His prospects also progressed more quickly to Grade Twelve, at which time they were more ready to fully embrace everything Lucan had to offer.

Once again, Marketing Mike had come up with the right idea. Even though most people are looking for the quick-fix pill, they are willing to buy the bigger solution if you take them through a process of self-discovery.

Why not try it? It just might work for you.

FOURTEEN

The Third Degree

One thing about business that is definitely not fun is The Third Degree. That's when you give a sales presentation to a room full of prospects, and then they pepper you with questions like

- Why should we pick your company as our supplier?
- What makes your products and services better than those of your competitors?
- What results have you achieved for your clients?
- How can you provide your services for the cheapest price?
- Are you available on weekends and at night if we need you?
- What exactly is your background, and why does that make you qualified for this project?

If you have ever been involved in sales or marketing, you know what I'm talking about. The Third Degree is hell on earth. You try to look calm and confident while the questions come at you like cluster bombs. Most of the time, you walk out of these dog-and-pony shows feeling more like a dog than a prize pony.

Speaking with Marketing Mike, I asked him if there was some way to handle The Third Degree more effectively.

"If you play The Third Degree game, you will hardly ever win," he explained. "And it will sap your confidence."

"Why's that?" I asked.

"Because when you give a presentation and prospects ask you these hard questions, you are on the defensive the whole time. You don't have a lot of power in the relationship."

"So how do you change the game?"

"You turn the tables," he answered. "You become a coach instead of a salesperson. You play The Coaching Sales Game."

"How does that work?"

"Before you go to the presentation, send out a questionnaire with a list of questions you want everyone to answer about the business. When you arrive at the meeting, explain that you don't have a presentation. Tell the group that you will conduct a workshop instead."

"You mean I shouldn't do a presentation at all?"

"That's right. Turn the tables on your prospects. Start asking them lots of questions about their business. Give them some exercises to do. Give them The Third Degree."

"What do you mean by exercises?"

"Create some worksheets that force your prospects to explain their goals, their challenges, and their plans for the future. Act like a coach instead of a salesperson."

"What's the difference between a coach and a salesperson?" I asked.

"A salesperson is someone who is expected to answer questions," Mike explained. "Salespeople think they will get the sale if they come up with really good answers. On the other hand, a coach is someone who asks really good questions. Coaches help people figure things out for themselves by leading them through a series of questions and exercises."

"Why is that a better way to do things?"

"Well," Marketing Mike began, once again finding the perfect example, "let's take a look at the job of a fitness coach. A fitness coach doesn't do the exercises. Instead, the coach tells the client what exercises to do, and encourages him to do the push-ups and sit-ups himself. As a result, the client gets into great shape."

"So you're saying that we should get our prospects and customers to do most of the work."

"That's right. Acting as a coach, you get the clients to do the thinking and the work that they need to do. You simply provide the questions and the exercises, along with lots of ideas and advice."

"Can you still give advice if you're a coach?"

"Absolutely! But you give advice in the form of options and possibilities. You simply give people information. They have to make up their own minds. This approach is much more powerful."

"So how can I get started?" I asked.

Over the next few hours, Marketing Mike stitched together a completely different way to handle The Third Degree. Although I was skeptical, I promised I would give it a try on my next prospect.

The prospect was Daynard Electronics. Daynard was looking for a marketing company to help them expand their business into new markets. I was invited to give a presentation to their marketing group. My company was one of seven agencies giving a pitch.

"Before I come to see you, I would like you to complete my questionnaire about your company and its goals," I told Miranda, the vice-president of new business development at Daynard. "If you and your team complete the questionnaire and send it to me, I can tailor the meeting to better suit your needs."

Miranda thought the questionnaire was a great idea. Every member of the team filled one out. The answers revealed dramatic differences. Already, I could see that the team members needed some coaching on the direction of their marketing plan.

I spent the night before the meeting with my

wife and kids. Normally, I would have been at the office slaving over my PowerPoint slides and support material. But now that I was a coach, not a salesperson, I didn't need to do that extra work.

The next morning, I showed up at Daynard Electronics and was ushered into a boardroom filled with an earnest, yet slightly glum, gaggle of middle managers. Having sat through five presentations that morning, they looked a little worn out.

I got right to it. "The first thing I want you to understand about me and my company is that we are different."

"Everybody says that," one of the middle managers shot back.

"Well, in my case it's true," I shot right back. "We aren't marketing consultants, we are marketing coaches. Instead of giving you a presentation, I am going to lead you through a series of marketing exercises."

"Aren't you going to give a presentation?" another middle manager asked.

"No. Instead of explaining what I do, I am just going to get started and do it with you. You will understand how I can help you better this way."

Although many of the middle managers were thrown off by my curveball, grudging assent was expressed around the table.

"Here is the first exercise," I began. "It is a scorecard to determine whether you have fallen into The Product-First Trap."

"What's The Product-First Trap?" someone asked.

"That's when you build your business around one or two products and services—and you can't get beyond them," I said. "The Product-First Trap stops you psychologically from creating more value for your customers."

"That sounds bad," someone said.

"It is," I agreed. "Lots of businesses get stuck in this trap. It saps their creativity and confidence."

Over the next thirty minutes, I helped them work through the questions on the scorecard. During this exercise, they came to the conclusion that they had a long way to go in the development of their marketing program.

"Now, I would like you to do this exercise to determine clear goals as a group," I summed up. "I would like you to write down what you would like to achieve over the next year from your marketing program."

I gave the team members ten minutes to write down their answers while I left the room. When I returned, I had each person explain what he or she had written.

"We would like to have twice the number of customers," one person said.

"We would like to triple our revenue from each customer," a second explained.

"We would like to lower our expenses by twenty percent," a third added.

While the team read out their goals, I recorded them on my laptop. When they were done, I read their collective marketing vision back to them. I could see immediately that they appeared more excited and motivated. They all looked more confident.

"Are you committed to achieving this vision?" I asked the group.

"Absolutely," they replied.

"Are you prepared to do what is necessary to achieve this vision?"

"Yes," they chorused.

"Would you like to hear about how I can help you achieve this vision?"

"Yes, indeed."

Over the next fifteen minutes, I explained how my company could help them realize these goals. I told them about the next phase: a three-hour planning session. The session would help them develop a strategic plan to achieve their goals.

Then I asked them if they felt they had made any progress during our initial session.

"We are much clearer about our current situation," Miranda said. "We are clearer about our goals. We are also more in sync as a team. This has been great. We would like to set up the next session."

Thrilled with the outcome, I called up Marketing Mike. "It worked," I said. "I turned the tables on them and gave them The Third Degree. And they loved it. But I'm still not sure I understand exactly why it worked."

"The Coaching Game works because you are putting the focus completely on the prospect and not on yourself," Marketing Mike explained. "Most people don't want to play the old game anymore, but they don't know anything else. By getting them started right away, they get a sense of immediate accomplishment. They also get to know you better and learn first-hand how you work. They experience directly what it is like to work with you. And, by playing The Coaching Game, you set yourself completely apart from the other companies that played the old sales game."

Mike's insights were illuminating. Since that time, I have played The Coaching Game with hundreds of prospects. A large number of them have become clients. And I no longer have to put up with The Third Degree.

And neither do you.

FIFTEEN

The Mountain Guide

Danny McNish, a senior partner at the design firm of Bodhead, Beaman & McNish, expressed dismay at a recent turn of events.

"I can't believe we didn't get the contract," he groaned. "They really needed our help. Their current design work is terrible."

"What happened?" I asked.

"We met with a prospect at their downtown offices," Danny began. "We spoke with their senior people, and they showed us their current brochure and Web site. I told them they needed to redo all their marketing material because it's awful. I told them they were projecting a poor image in the marketplace."

"What was their reaction?" I asked.

"They got really defensive. They were insulted because I thought their stuff was unprofessional. But it was. I was doing them a favour. They really need help."

"Then what happened?"

"Well, they ended the meeting abruptly. They

said they wanted to think about it. But when I called back, no one wanted to speak to me. They wouldn't return my calls."

"I suppose they were unhappy about your comments."

"I guess. But I was just telling them the truth—my honest opinion. Isn't that what a consultant is supposed to do?"

On leaving my lunch with Danny, I told him I would have a meeting with Marketing Mike and get his opinion.

"Do you think a salesperson should tell people the whole truth about their current situation?" I asked my mentor.

"Honesty is very important, but you have to be judicious in applying it," he explained in his typical matter-of-fact way, "or you will really turn people off."

"What do you mean by that?"

"Well," Marketing Mike began, coming up with an illustration, "let's pretend you're a mountain guide on Mount Everest. You have a specialty. You take people from halfway up Mount Everest to the top. In order to work with you, people have to climb halfway on their own or with the help of someone else."

"Okay, I can picture that."

"So a climber makes it halfway up, but he doesn't know any better, so he starts climbing the second half on his own. You shout at him, and tell him to stop because the second half of the mountain is much more dangerous than the first half. You tell him it is steeper, the air is thinner, there are constant avalanches, and a lot of people die up there."

"That sounds scary," I said.

"That's the idea. You have to scare him or he'll go up on his own and probably kill himself."

"But isn't that what Danny McNish told his prospects—that they needed his help to get to the top of the mountain?"

"Well, he got only part of it right. Ask yourself, what's the problem with making the climber too scared?"

"I guess if he's too scared, he won't go up at all. He'll be paralyzed by fear."

"That's right. And it's not good for your business if everyone is too scared to climb the second half of Mount Everest."

"So what do you do?"

"You tell the climber that he can make it to the top, with a little help, because he has already demonstrated skill, courage, persistence, and strength. These are all important attributes that will help him get to the top."

"So you're saying we should flatter our prospects?"

"Not really," Marketing Mike corrected me. "But before we weigh in with our criticisms, we should first acknowledge all the things they have done right so far. We should help the prospects see how they are already halfway up their mountain."

"How will this help me in a sales situation?" I asked.

"It will help," Marketing Mike explained, "because you and your prospect will realize together what they've already accomplished and where they should go next. You will have identified their growth edge."

"What's a 'growth edge'?"

"It's the exact place where a person needs help. For example, if you teach *See Spot Run* to a kid in Grade Six, he will be bored silly. If you try to teach the same kid nuclear physics, he won't understand it. You have to determine the kid's growth edge and tailor your instruction to match his level. Otherwise, your help will be useless."

"So what did Danny McNish do so terribly wrong?"

"I think his prospects were insulted because Danny didn't acknowledge that they were halfway up the mountain. He told them they were at the bottom of the mountain, and he was there to save them."

"So you think he came across as a know-it-all?"

"Absolutely. I'm sure Danny was trying to help them by being honest, but it backfired. The prospects would have responded more favourably if he had told them first off what they had done right. Obviously, they had already invested a lot of time and money. They didn't want to hear that they needed to start at the bottom of the mountain again."

"But what if it's true, that they are really at the

bottom of Mount Everest?"

"It doesn't matter who you're talking to. Everyone is halfway up a mountain. You just have to look harder to find out what they've accomplished, no matter how small or seemingly insignificant."

Marketing Mike's advice had a profound impact on Danny McNish. He realized immediately that he had been coming across as arrogant and conde-scending.

"That approach isn't going to help me get cus-tomers," Danny acknowledged. "I need to start looking for my prospect's growth edge."

I was also genuinely changed by Marketing Mike's insight. As a coach, I now begin by looking for my prospect's growth edge in their marketing program. Before giving advice, I seek first to recog-nize and applaud what they have done right so far. This simple advice has helped me start many new business relationships.

So what about you? Do you think your prospects are winners or losers? Ask yourself this question. The answer may help change your business for the better.

SIXTEEN

The Dating Game

As the sales manager at Pyromania Inc., the country's leading fireworks distributor, Tiffany Stokes and her team had failed once again to meet their quarterly sales quota. Expressing her deep frustration, Tiffany aired her complaints.

"We aren't getting to see enough prospects," she said. "And we aren't closing enough sales. We're obviously doing something wrong, but I'm not sure what it is."

"How do you go about getting prospects and making sales?" I asked Tiffany.

"Well," she replied, "we have a database of prospects, most of them retailers. We call them and set up appointments. Then we meet with them and try to close the sale."

"How many calls do you have to make to set up one appointment?"

"We usually have to call ten prospects to set up one appointment," she explained.

"And what do you do at the sales presentation?"

"We have a little chit-chat. Then we present our

line of fireworks and discuss pricing. If things go well, we get out the contract and sign the deal."

"So you're finding that this method does not work very well."

"Sometimes it works," she said, "but most of the time, the prospect backs away and doesn't buy. And when we call them later on, it is like we had never met."

"That doesn't sound good," I told her.

"If you can think of a better way to sell fireworks, we would be most thankful."

I told Tiffany that I would give her problem some deep thought and get back to her with an answer. Of course, I immediately picked up the telephone and called Marketing Mike.

After I filled him in, Marketing Mike summed up the difficulty. "It's not working because she is proposing marriage on the first date!"

"What do you mean by that?" I asked him.

"It's helpful to think of sales as a Dating Game," Marketing Mike explained. "Just like romantic dating, sales dating is about developing trust, intimacy, and communication. And most important of all, it's about time."

"Can you explain that a little more?"

"Of course. Let's think about dating. If you were looking for a mate, you'd first have to find some prospects. You'd find prospects by getting a referral from a friend, advertising in the relationships-wanted section of the newspaper, joining an on-line dating service, or getting out and meeting people."

"That's hard."

"You're right. Finding a prospective mate is hard, but it's usually better than being lonely."

"That's for sure. Okay," I went on, "so now that you've found someone, then what?"

"Then the next step, of course, is to ask the person out on a date."

"I hate doing that."

"Why?"

"Because I'm afraid they'll reject me, and I'll feel like a loser."

"You'll be a loser only if you don't ask them out on a date. If they say no, then at least you tried."

"I agree with you."

"So," Marketing Mike went on, "what do you think you can do to increase the chances that the prospect will agree to the date?"

"Well, I suppose I should start by making sure I look good."

"That's a start. But you also have to make the date sound like a good time."

"What do you mean?"

"You could suggest going out to a nice restaurant, and then out for dancing at the hottest club in town. Doesn't that sound better than a grilled cheese sandwich at the local diner?"

"It sure does! So then what?"

"So let's assume the person accepts the date. Now we're on the date. Everything is going great.

Amazing dinner. Lots of good discussion. You're hitting it off. And then you pull out a ring and propose marriage. How does that sound?"

"That would be really dumb."

"Why?"

"Because it's too early in the relationship to propose marriage?"

"Why?"

"Because your date would think that you're coming on too strong—and that you're really desperate. They just aren't ready for such a proposal."

"Why?"

"Because they don't know you well enough. They haven't spent enough time with you. They don't know if they can trust you."

"Exactly. But that's what most salespeople do. They propose marriage on the first date. They pull out the contract and expect the prospect to sign."

"No wonder Tiffany and her team aren't making enough sales," I said as the proverbial light bulb lit up.

"That's right. Tiffany needs to slow down the process and do some courting first before she proposes marriage. She's trying to light the fireworks before the sun goes down."

"So what should Tiffany do instead?" I asked.

"Two things," Marketing Mike began. "She will get more dates with prospects if she makes the first date sound more interesting."

"How can she do that?"

"She should repackage the first date as a special event that will help the retailer figure out how to sell more fireworks. She could bring in retail promotion experts who can explain how to merchandise the fireworks more effectively."

"That sounds like a more interesting date," I said.

"Then she could slow down the sales process by not pressing for a sale right away."

"But what if the retailer wants to buy the fireworks right then and there?"

"That's okay. But it has to be the retailer's idea. You have to feel out the situation. If you come on too strong, the retailer will back away. If you act casual and relaxed, the retailer might be the one who makes the proposal."

"So you don't want to look too eager?"

"Exactly. If you look too eager to get married right away, the prospect will get scared and run off."

Armed with this pearl of wisdom, I spoke to Tiffany and her group about the subtle art of sales dating.

"You're absolutely right," Tiffany proclaimed. "We've been coming on too strong. And we haven't been making our dates sound very interesting."

Over the next quarter, sales at Pyromania Inc. started to explode. By following the rules of The Dating Game, Tiffany and her sales force became more relaxed and patient. They learned to read the feelings of their prospects more precisely. They didn't try to close the sale immediately if the prospect seemed uncertain. They took their time. And as a result, they started to make more sales and even bigger sales.

So think about your sales methods. Are you offering your prospects a grilled cheese sandwich or a night at the best bistro in town? Are you pulling out the ring and proposing on the first date? Are you coming on too strong?

If you answered yes to one or more of these questions, then remember what you've just read. Playing The Dating Game could increase your sales and make you more money.

SEVENTEEN

The Forest

Raising his voice to drown out the clamour coming from a massive recycling machine, Tanner Bryson bellowed, "The 4000XT can sort and recycle more than ten tonnes of industrial waste per hour."

"That's quite impressive," I bellowed back. "What kind of material does it recycle?"

"Anything that's left over from the demolition of an industrial building," Tanner shouted proudly. "We extract lots of highly valuable stuff from this waste: steel, copper, magnesium, silver—and lots of other things."

Following the tour of his plant, Tanner invited me back to his office to discuss his business in a more quiet setting.

"Recyclo-Link has been in operation for two years now," Tanner said. "And we have attracted lots of great customers. But we want to grow faster— a lot faster."

"How fast do you want to grow?"

"I want to make my company ten times bigger over the next three years."

"That's really ambitious," I said. "How fast has your business grown so far?"

"Well, that's the thing. We've been growing at a snail's pace. At this rate, it's going to take a thousand years to expand our business ten times. Do you have any suggestions on how we can accelerate our growth?"

"I'll mull over your situation and report back in a few days," I told Tanner.

The next day, I drove out to Marketing Mike's tree reserve in the country. Marketing Mike had purchased the property twelve years ago as a getaway from the city. When I arrived, I was astounded by the beauty and scope of his tree sanctuary.

"We've got more than 10 000 trees on the property," Marketing Mike explained. "When we bought the place, this was just flat, barren farmland. Now we have a forest."

Walking along a trail through groves of towering maple, pine, cedar, spruce, and larch, I told Marketing Mike about Tanner Bryson and his frustration. "He really wants to super-charge his company and get a lot bigger quickly. I don't know if he can do it, but I admire his drive and ambition."

"Yes, Tanner's goals are admirable," Marketing Mike said, while clearing away a mound of leaves that were choking a tiny sapling. "But I think Tanner needs to look at the growth of his business in a different way."

"How's that?" I asked.

"Well, let's use this forest as an example. Twelve years ago, I had a dream of growing a forest in the country. As I said, when I bought this land it was a flat farmer's field. You could see clear across the county from where we are standing right now."

"I can't imagine it."

"Well, twelve years ago you could not imagine this forest either."

"So how did you get it started?"

"We planted more than 10,000 trees over a period of two weeks. They weren't any bigger than the little cedar sapling right here."

"That sounds like a lot of work."

"The planting was just the beginning of it. Then we had to keep cutting the grass around the seedlings to give them light and water."

"For how long did you have to do that?" I asked.

"For about four years. It was back-breaking work. We also had to fight off the animals that wanted to gnaw at the bark. And we replaced all the seedlings that didn't survive."

"Wow," I replied, impressed.

"Then we had to face all the criticism and skepticism," Marketing Mike said.

"What kind of criticism?"

"Very few people believed in my vision. The farmers thought I was crazy to waste good farmland on a bunch of trees. My friends laughed at my tiny seedlings when I described my dream of a giant forest. They just couldn't see my vision. They said it would take a hundred years to turn the little trees into a forest."

"So what did you do?"

"I blocked out their derision and continued to visualize my ultimate picture of the forest. The image sustained me. It kept me working during those hard initial years. Then something miraculous happened."

"What?"

"Around the fifth year, the trees started to grow at an incredible rate. All of a sudden, they were taller than I was. In the sixth year, we started cutting trails between the trees. In the seventh year, some of the trees were more than twenty feet tall."

"That's astounding. Why did they suddenly start growing so fast?"

"Trees grow exponentially," Mike explained. "At first they are just getting established and the growth seems minuscule, about a couple of inches a year. But when they reach a certain size, the trees are more established. They start to grow by one or two feet a year, and suddenly you have a forest."

"What did all the farmers and your friends think?"

"They were flabbergasted. They couldn't understand what had happened. It was very satisfying."

"So what does this forest have to do with Tanner Bryson and his recycling company?"

"You tell me," Marketing Mike said with a twinkle in his eye.

"I guess Tanner is being too impatient. He just planted his trees two years ago, and he wants them to become a forest too soon."

"That's exactly it," Marketing Mike agreed. "He is trying to turn little saplings into giant redwoods overnight. And it isn't going to work out that way."

"What if he tries to grow his business too fast?" I asked.

"If he tries to grow his business faster than is natural, he could destroy the whole operation."

"How would that happen?"

"So many companies grow too quickly, before they have their systems and processes perfected. They don't bother to tend each little tree. So when their business grows, it reaches a critical point. Imperfections and a lack of integrated processes become major problems. Often the business collapses at the moment when its growth seems most spectacular."

"That sounds terrible," I said. "So what do you think Tanner should do to grow his business?"

"He should remember that you don't grow a forest overnight. He should focus on tending each individual seedling. In other words, he should perfect and hone all his systems and procedures. He should stay focused on his vision, and not be beaten down by the skepticism and impatience of others. He should revel in the joy of creating something built to last. And before you know it, his business will start to bloom naturally. If he keeps nurturing his trees, he will have the forest he is dreaming about."

Driving away from Marketing Mike's tree sanctuary, I had a completely different perspective on Tanner's business. I shared this story with Tanner, and he quickly grasped the moral of the tale.

"You are right," he said. "My business is like a tree sanctuary. These are the early years. I have a lot of work to do, but the effort will pay off. I just have to keep at it and not let other people convince me that there is some way to get rich quick. I know that this business will grow. I just have to let it happen naturally."

It was a revelation that proved prophetic. In Tanner's sixth year of business, his fortunes soared. By working hard to develop well-refined systems and procedures first, he was able to open three new recycling plants in other countries. He was able to license his methodologies to other recycling companies. He also felt more confident that his forest would continue to grow during his lifetime, and beyond.

So, here are some questions: Are you trying to grow your business too fast, without tending to your seedlings first? Are you letting the disbelief of others cloud your vision and leach your confidence? If so, remember the story of The Forest. It may give you strength during the early stages of your business.

The Mystery of Marketing Mike

Who is Marketing Mike?

The answer to this has become the stuff of myth and legend. Some people believe Marketing Mike is a fanciful but benign character like Santa Claus or the Easter Bunny. Because some people claim to have seen or met him, others compare Marketing Mike to Bigfoot or the Loch Ness monster. Others cry hoax, claiming Marketing Mike is simply a fictitious person Bill Bishop concocted to facilitate his book's narrative.

So what is the answer to this riddle? What's the real truth? Got to know? Eternally curious? Can't sleep?

Visit www.biginc.com. All will be revealed.

ACKNOWLEDGEMENTS

Behind the Lobster Tale

Although Marketing Mike's assistance has been the backbone of my career, and the chief inspiration for this book, I would be remiss if I did not extend my appreciation to scores of individuals who have had a profound influence on me. Every one of them has given me gifts too numerous to enumerate properly.

My wife, Ginny, is the nurturer of my soul and the challenger of my often distended ego. Her psychological insights and healing spirit give me direction and strength when I most need it.

My father, Arthur, and my mother, Priscilla— the pubescent Frog and Bunny debacle notwithstanding—taught me about the fun world of business and marketing. Our classroom was the kitchen table.

My children, Douglas and Robin, still teach me that no matter how old I get there is always something new to learn.

Thanks to my confrères at the office: Curtis Verstraete, Erin James, Corey Kilmartin, Bonnie Werezak, George McClellan, and Sean Wenzel. And a special *merci beaucoup* to John Beauchamp, who has freed up a million minutes of my time so I can indulge my fanciful literary pursuits.

I would also like to thank my sister, Diana, Dan Liebman, and Janie Yoon for meticulously editing the text of this book.

Thanks, too, to my business and marketing coaches over the years: the managers at the steak restaurant, who dragged me out of the kitchen into the scary but exhilarating world of waitering; Peter Creaghan, my magazine publishing partner, who taught me the fine art of the two-man sale; the sales squad at *Toronto Life* magazine, who helped me understand the fascinating world of magazine publishing; Brian Chadderton, my mentor at Berger & Associates, who generously shared his vast knowledge of publicity and public relations.

I would also like to offer my thanks to the thousands of clients who have put their trust in my advice and services over the past decades. Every one of them has taught me something about business. They have forced me to challenge my own ideas and assumptions. They have compelled me to improve constantly; to always strive for something better; to look at creativity and innovation as a perpetual motion machine; and, most importantly, to view work, business, and life as roads best travelled with a spirit of adventure, fraternity, conviviality, and fun.

And last, but certainly not least, I want to thank *you* for taking the time to read this book. Writing *How to Sell a Lobster* has been its own reward, but if you have gleaned even one smidgen of useful advice or insight from this tome, then I am most indisputably gratified.

About the Author

BILL BISHOP is the CEO of Bishop Information Group Inc., a marketing and communications consulting company located in Toronto, Canada. Since he was eight years old, Bill has had more than 100 jobs; he has consulted with more than 4000 companies during his multi-faceted career. He lives in Toronto with his wife and two kids, four cats, and numerous tropical fish.